AF492920

The New Scramble for Africa

By Keidi Awadu for the
Conscious Rasta Press
and Black Star Media Global

Published by the Conscious
Rasta Press
9515 W. Cherrydale Ct.
Las Vegas NV 89147

For interview inquies contact 323.902.2919 (Pacific)

Email to keidi@libradio.net

See the catalog at www.Keidi.biz/CRP2012

Copyright July 2015 by Keidi Awadu for the Conscious Rasta Press

Contents

Chapter 1 – Introduction

This book has been particularly challenging for me to complete for several reasons. The first of which is because I am so busy engaging such a broad spectrum of activities that are a resulting consequence of constant research, study, and having to create an engaging daily Internet radio broadcast. Quite simply, when you are in a position to inform the world frequently covering the spectrum of major and minor changes which are taking place that will have a great impact on the future, it can also provoke the feeling that you *have to* do something about what you are discovering to be a part of the community that is positively influencing the future outcome.

Second, as many of you know, I wear a lot of hats, one of which is that of an author. This particular profession of investigative journalism requires a lot of research, writing, fact-checking, editing, and, as I am independently publishing as well, it involves formatting the books and raising funds to get the printing and marketing done.

Further, in addition to journalism, I manage other crafts and enterprises as well: that of filmmaker, musician, nutritional health consultant, raw food chef, lecturer, and graphics artist. Some of these keep me on the road for many weeks during the year.

Third, I am challenged continuously toward ongoing study and research for my own personal growth, knowledge mastery and accreditation. Each year I try to take at least one college-administered online course (though I have never formally enrolled in a university, I have used campus resources for study all my life) and have acquired two certifications so far, one in Childhood Nutrition, and another in Global Health Strategies. As I write I am about to embark on another such online course: *Growing Entrepreneurship in Transitioning Economies*.

The information that has been compiled for this edition of the *Conscious Rasta Report*, has been amassed over the course of decades; the Ebola research itself comprises unique investigative research that I conducted more than 20 years ago. Yet, a significant amount of this particular Report must be as up-to-date as possible. Economic, business, investment and development trends, because of their ever-changing nature, need to be as close to cutting edge as possible for our most advantageous position. Thus the dilemma presents itself when I commit to finish authoring a book, work on the editing process, creating the graphics, formatting and publishing, that at a point further incoming research data must be filed away for future reporting. With regard to the information contained herein, I am already at a point where another significant work will have to fill in the gap of just the last few months that it has taken to get this book completed.

Much of my newest work centers on this compelling fascination with the theme of *Africa Rising*. I first developed a huge awareness of this theme in the latter part of 2014, when the final focus on completing this book was a priority. By March of 2015, I became so obsessed with this new theme that I committed an entire month of intense research instruction broadcasting to share what I was finding with as many as would be interested. By the end of that month's collection of over 50 hours of broadcast recordings, I had firmly declared that we are presently witnessing (at least those who have the foresight to commit their attention) the *rebirth of great civilization* on the African continent; a truly historic event that would impact world affairs for centuries to come.

The spectrum of trends which have brought Africa Rising to this impressive stage is so broad and detailed that it will undeniably take another complete book for me to effectively share the mass of data that I have been examining. Suffice to say, when that book has been written, because of the pace of changes which are taking place, the world's power locus will already be shifting and transforming whole regions quite significantly.

With regard to this Report, it is by no means close to obsolescence. The book begins with an examination of the reappearance of the Ebola pandemic that, according to my radical hypothesis, is much more of a *political* threat to the affected nations than one of public health.

How America has used these Ebola crises (and as you will learn, quite likely was the instigator of the disease as well) to push for medical and pharmaceutical hegemony over the rapidly growing population of the African continent, is something that we had best understand if we are to have any chance at all to beat them to their goal. America is not the only country scrambling to be chief provider of pharmaceutical drugs and other medical technologies to an African continent whose population will reach over 2 billion by 2050.

From the August 2014 US-Africa Summit, which took place in Washington, DC, and which involved heads of state and top officials from 50 African nations, we also have some critical revelations about security policies as well as a self-serving plan for youth leadership development. What came out of that summit in terms of operational programs and policies is something that we absolutely should be carefully scrutinizing.

Therefore, this book is intended to be simultaneously: 1) a primer on the current status of Pan African economics and development; 2) a warning to our "culturally conscious community" that significant changes are taking place for which far too many of us are nearly completely oblivious; 3) a correction of much of the disinformation that is continuously propagated regarding Africa, its people, and development; 4) as well as a futurist projection which projects the outcome of current policies and practices that will have a powerful long-term impact on global issues.

I intend to stir within each reader the same burning passion that I have for Pan African affairs, politics, culture, economics, and development. With such a driving motivation, you will likely also commence to research and confirm for yourself what is truth or falsehood within the mass of news that we get about Africa. You may also decide that you, too, want to involve yourself in assisting this phenomenon of Africa Rising.

You do also want to travel to the African continent as soon and as often as possible. A number of us have visited our African homeland, and this is an empowering trend. It is in regular travel to the continent that we get our most visionary work accomplished. We discover that we become more deeply engaged in personal relationships as well as adept at business ventures. Those with a strong entrepreneurial spirit cannot help but bear witness to the large spectrum of opportunities which abound within African nations.

Another great benefit of such travel is that we start to recreate Africa culturally within our own lives when we return from such journeys. We decorate our homes with magnificent African art, wear the beautiful garbs we have retrieved, tune into the music and news stories about those areas which we have witnessed ourselves. One of the best outcomes for me has been a heightened ability to encounter continental-born Africans here in the US and to readily relate to them. Thus I can enjoy the opportunity to return to them some of the wonderful hospitality that I have *always* been shown during my African travels.

"The future belongs to those who are prepared to create it today." Yet the logic of this statement is undeniable. I am a futurist, having incorporated at least 9 separate disciplines which encompass the field. I have witnessed the future clearly enough to want to chart a firm course into the future so that my children, our children, and the generations to follow will be primary beneficiaries of our varied investments.

Upon reading this book I trust that you will be further prepared, highly motivated and excited by keen insights into those things that will transform and define the future. At some point during this *paradigm shift*, you may believe and act as I have done with regard to these key insights regarding future trends.

Armed with right and correct information, having gathered together critical resources that are required for manifesting our own sovereign development and autonomy, we are now charged with the mission of taking firm control of our own course of development. We must further stabilize our families and communities, collaborate to bring available natural resources (including *human capital*) to their fullest potential, elevate a robust group economy, engage in international trade, educate ourselves to power from pre-school to career upgrade, and to find a means to secure everything we do without being bullied by outsiders or collaborators that they would develop within our midst.

So, prepare yourself for this magnificent journey. There is indeed so much reason to be excited, optimistic, and motivated toward action. African affairs and leadership have profoundly influenced the world. This is true today and will be *increasingly* relevant for the next 85 years and more. Let's make sure that each of us moves to become key orchestrators of this global transformation.

So...are you ready to get this party started?

Chapter 2 – Ebola's Shadow Hanging Over Africa

It is extremely critical to the foundational theme of this book that I begin by returning to my extensive 1995 inquiry into Ebola Zaire. This massive investigative report appeared in. my 1997 book, **Conspiracies and High Crimes**. The chapter was entitled, EBOLA: Virus Outbreak or Mycotoxin Attack? There was just so much valuable research that I amassed for the Report. It explored the history, as well as the current state of chemical, biological, and toxin warfare, along with implications for the future. By the conclusion of that report I had become, and remain, quite confident that the idea of an infectious virus causing the hemorrhaging effects being reported was incorrect. I believe it was a new state of toxin warfare that was imposed.

The topic of Ebola has so captivated the attention of so many of us who have come under significant influence from the news coverage it has recently received. Therefore, I wish to begin this publication with my highly researched perspective. As the topic returned in early August 2014 to become an hourly obsession with a spectrum of media outlets, I was for a while reluctant to get deeply engaged as I had already covered this 19 years ago in much depth and, to be quite frank, have grown tired of talking about a problem that had already been resolved within my frame of references.

Nonetheless, media hype and hysteria continued for months (and is just tapering off as I write four months later), and I increasingly agreed to do radio interviews as well as set aside a brief portion of my frequent lectures and workshops to the topic of Ebola.

So let me share portions of my 20-year-old investigation into Ebola and help you to understand why I could not get too overly excited with this current, almost hysterical, obsession with "infectious diseases" from Africa as projected from the perspective of western healthcare agencies and corporate media.

In the spring of 1994, much attention was focused on a massive health crisis happening in the central African nation of Zaire (since renamed the Democratic Republic of the Congo). According to widespread accounts, the Democratic Republic of the Congo was suffering its third reported outbreak of the "deadly virus" Ebola. The suspect viral agent, first identified during a reported 1976 outbreak in a rural section of the country, was named after the Ebola River in northern DR Congo.[1]

Within my extensive research study, I painstakingly examined all available details of that case as they were widely published through the press and merged that information with my deep inquiry into the modern state of biological and chemical warfare (CBW) and a third class of CBW called "toxin warfare." In particular, concerning Ebola, toxin warfare became the center of my focus because it facilitates the use of offensive weapons agents that could be handled with the security of chemical weapons yet whose symptoms resemble those of infectious diseases. People should recognize the impact of naturally produced toxins on health with an understanding of the dangerous and often life-threatening impact of bites from snakes and spiders, frog venom as well as toxins produced by pathogenic bacteria. *Biological toxins* are chemicals that are manufactured by or are a byproduct of living organisms. [2]

---

[1] CONSPIRACIES AND HIGH CRIMES by Keidi Obi Awadu, Conscious Rasta Press, Vol 5 No 3, Oct. 1998

[2] GENE WARS: MILITARY CONTROL OVER THE NEW GENETIC TECHNOLOGIES by Charles Piller and Keith R. Yamamoto, Beech Tree Books, William Morrow, New York, pg 22

As stated, that particular report, **entitled EBOLA: Virus Outbreak or Mycotoxin Attack**," appeared in the more extensive 1998 Conscious Rasta Report entitled *CONSPIRACIES AND HIGH CRIMES*. Key findings from that report included the following essential points:

- Since the renunciation of *biological* warfare under the administration of Richard Nixon, research on a broad spectrum of biological, chemical and toxin agents has continued at an estimated two dozen facilities across the U.S. under the guise that the studies were being conducted to develop defensive techniques against CBW agents;

- Among the many "virus weapons" that were reportedly stored in the U.S. arsenal at the U.S. Army Medical Research Institute of Infectious Diseases (USAMRIID) at Ft. Detrick, Maryland, were some *hemorrhagic viruses* (reported to be *bleeding* diseases) including Ebola, Lassa fever, Marburg fever, Junin, Machupo, and Congo-Crimean hemorrhagic fever. Other deadly pathogens said to have been in storage at USAMRIID included Rift Valley fever, West Nile encephalitis, Orapouche fever, and others.

- One of the oldest diseases known to humanity, *Ergot,* resulted from food poisoning caused by a fungus that grew on moldy, poorly-stored grains, and spoiled bread. It was the deadly effect of a mycotoxin (fungus toxin) produced by a class of bacteria called *Fusarium*. [3] The impact of poisoning from this fungal toxin has been called various names throughout history, including "Saint Vitus's dance," "Saint Anthony's fire," and epilepsy. Symptoms of the poisoning

---

[3] YELLOW RAIN: A JOURNEY THROUGH THE TERROR OF CHEMICAL WARFARE, by Sterling Seagrave. Pgs 185-189

often included blindness, dementia, plague, extensive bleeding, and more. In the book **YELLOW RAIN: A Journey Through the Terror of Chemical Warfare**, author Sterling Seagrave wrote:

> "Ergot was only one of the fungal poisons—or mycotoxins… It was, above all, a bleeding disease. Minutes after the poisoned grain was eaten, the victim began to burn in the mouth, throat, esophagus, and stomach, as the poison quickly went to work on the mucous membranes, causing surface hemorrhages. Then came a hemorrhagic rash on the skin of the chest, spreading within the hour to the abdomen, legs, arms and face. The rapid onslaught of internal bleeding was accompanied by violent headaches, dizziness, vertigo, weakness and fatigue, fever, sweating, angina, neurological tremors spasms and then convulsions. The blood pressure fell, bleeding became heavy in the intestines and all the vital organs and glands— particularly in the adrenal and thyroid glands, gonads, uterus, and pleura. Suddenly, the lungs gushed blood, filling quickly with it… In the few cases where people survived, there was blood seeping from the eyes and ears—and all other orifices…"

- Following a massive outbreak of Ergot in the Soviet Union during the 1930s, it is believed that Russian scientists began studying one particular type of these mycotoxin poison types, *trichothecenes* (or T2 toxins).   American researchers presumed that the Soviets had weaponized T2, and there were reports that it was used to deadly effect on populations in Laos, Kampuchea (Cambodia), and Afghanistan.

- Many published reports are alleging the use of chem-bio warfare agents. The United States has been the country most frequently accused of using such weapons. At least nine countries are on record among those who suspected that their populations suffered at the hands of U.S. CBW offenses.[4]

- There is a class of bacteria called *coccidioides* to which it is often reported that people of African genetic descent are much more susceptible than are whites. Thus, the creation of so-called "Ethnic Weapons" has long been a consideration for CBW researchers. [5] As one published article revealed in 1970: "Coccidioides immititis is a fungus that causes coccidioidomycosis, commonly called 'Valley fever'... Valley fever is a systemic, sometimes fatal disease that the military has studied as a potential BW agent from the 1940s to the present. Blacks are up to ten times as likely to die from the disease as whites. ¶ Advances in biotechnology and human genetics have made the prospect of identifying these discriminating agents far easier than ever before..." [6]

- After examining many dozens of media reports, my analysis concluded that in the aftermath of an outbreak of the water-borne disease *shigella* earlier that year in the DR Congo, a shipment of U.S.-manufactured medical supplies was flown into the country which contained substances contaminated with the suspect "Ebola" toxin agent. To account for the distinctions between the increased delay in onset of symptoms, I hypothesized that this was a genetically altered form of T2 trichothecene that had been combined with a more innocuous bacteria such as e. Coli to facilitate

---

[4] GENE WARS, ibid, pgs 20-21
[5] ETHNIC WEAPONS by Carl A. Larson, Military Review, November 1970, pg 3
[6] GENE WARS, pg 100

production and ease of handling. It was within a month after this shipment of medical supplies arrived in Zaire that the Ebola outbreak was identified in the region.

There was so much more to this extensive, highly-referenced investigative report. To this day, I believe it to be the most comprehensive and explosive revelation on what has taken place concerning the history of Ebola outbreaks across Africa. If my assertions are correct, then any nation that would harbor and even deploy such a toxin weapon would logically have the antidote, or *anti-toxin serum*, in its storage as well.

With the latest news about an Ebola outbreak now encompassing as many as six or more nations, and two affected Americans receiving a so-called "experimental drug" as part of their successful treatment, this leads me to not only believe further that there is a serum for the deadly mycotoxin.

Yet I suspect that there is another more sinister agenda rising behind the scenes. Western drug companies seek to further impose medical-pharmaceutical hegemony over vulnerable and dependent nations that have rapidly expanding population numbers.

Chapter 3 – African Nations in Crisis and the West

We now arrive at a discussion of the persistent underdevelopment and continuing dependence of far too many African nations. Countries on the forefront of this current episode of Ebola outbreak include Guinea, Liberia, Sierra Leone, Senegal, and Nigeria while World Health Organization (WHO) authorities are suggesting that this could further spread to other West African nations such as Ghana, Togo, and Cote d'Ivoire.

Those of us who have engaged in in-depth background research on the political and economic histories of these countries recognize that there are lingering dependencies that make these nations more susceptible to manipulation from former colonial powers as well as internal and external factors that have allowed for insecurity and poor healthcare infrastructure.

There is a long and disturbing record of intrigue involving these nations and military intervention from the U.S., France, and the U.K., among others. As well, we've documented disruptive interaction with the UN agencies such as the WHO (the so-called AIDS *pandemic* is one such intrusive example), the International Monetary Fund and World Bank, multinational corporations, resource-extraction interests, and telecommunications companies – all indicate to this researcher that there is a renewed "mad scramble for Africa" taking place.

These African countries are made more vulnerable because of their extensive relations and interaction with their former colonial masters as well as the lingering legacy of the so-called "Cold War" wherein global economic competition between western capitalist nations was pitted against the bloc of socialist countries. Across

Africa, the "Cold War" was quite hot. Millions of Africans were killed, maimed, lives disrupted, made refugees, and otherwise severely disaffected because of the machinations of East versus West struggle for world economic dominance.

In August 2014, the US-African Summit was hosted in the American capital by the Obama administration to which some four dozen African heads of state attended. Notably, only two high profile state dinners were being hosted for individual African heads of state. The first of these two privileged leaders was Alassane Ouattara, the President of Cote d'Ivoire, recently installed through the heavy hand of French intervention after a disputed election and subsequent military coup.

The second specially-honored guest was Nigeria's President, Dr. Goodluck Ebele Azikiwe Jonathan, himself closely allied to President Obama along with the U.S. based petroleum corporations that dominate his nation's energy sector. These two countries also happened to be in the midst of the current Ebola cycle in West Africa.   It could be that the close relationship between the leaders of Cote d'Ivoire and Nigeria and the U.S. could lead to speculation on just how the Ebola pandemic has become so closely associated with their populations.

Chapter 4 – The Grand Chessboard

Such crises compel us to comprehend precisely how jockeying for power over African development and dominance over natural resources has evolved. As well, we would best seek to understand how this is expected to continue evolving over the coming decades and beyond. There has been much concern over the development of a "New World Order" within the circles of conspiracy research and dialog. According to this author, a large number of those engaging the topic have a superficial or simplistic understanding as to how this global competition is evolving. There are many great and small minds describing the transition of nations and the evolution of civilizations. Where do we turn for accurate and usable research?

What follows is a description of a seminal book by former U.S. National Security Council Advisor Zbigniew Brzezinski. This is the man credited as being the insider who shepherded the career of an obscure Occidental College student named Barack Obama through his university studies, into the Senate and up to occupying the most desired office in the world:

The Grand Chessboard: American Primacy and Its Geostrategic Imperatives is one of the major works of Zbigniew Brzezinski. Brzezinski graduated with a Ph.D. from Harvard University in 1953 and became Professor of American Foreign Policy at Johns Hopkins University before becoming the United States National Security Advisor during 1977—1981 under the administration of President Jimmy Carter.

Regarding the landmass of Eurasia as the center of global power, Brzezinski sets out to formulate a Eurasian geostrategy for the United States. In particular, he writes, it is imperative that no Eurasian challenger should emerge capable of dominating Eurasia and thus also of challenging America's global pre-eminence.

Much of his analysis is concerned with geostrategy in Central Asia, focusing on the exercise of power on the Eurasian landmass in a post-Soviet environment. In his chapter dedicated to what he refers to as the "Global Balkans," Brzezinski makes use of Halford J. Mackinder's Heartland Theory. [7]

It might be stated that "The Grand Chessboard" is an outdated strategy to control Eurasia as part of a plan for world domination, formulated more than a century ago. Still, I would like my readers to comprehend that such grandiose strategic positioning is a regular part of the business of governance from the perspective of the oligarchic elite who continually dominate global policies. There have been other such schemes before Brzezinski's vision, and several since. In more recent decades, we have witnessed the rapid emergence of China from their desperate status following the devastation in WWII and subsequent civil war against the Chinese Nationalists. That long struggle culminated in the "Cultural War." Now the world is amazed at China's steady emergence from centuries of political and economic colonization, which was followed by decades of isolationism. As I write, it is just announced this week that, in terms of *purchasing power*, China is the number one economy in the world, surpassing the European Union and the United States.

---

[7] THE GRAND CHESSBOARD, from Wikipedia, the free encyclopedia

Chapter 5 – Containing China

China has overtaken many former world powers in developing the largest economy on the planet and surpassed predictions to so rapidly overtake the number one spot held by the U.S. since the end of WWII. Across the African continent, one can readily and easily see evidence of this Chinese industrial behemoth carving out its access to resources needed to sustain such a rapid scale of industrial production. While many have grave concerns as to whether or not the Chinese are merely assuming the same position that European colonial powers have occupied within African territories over past centuries, there is great excitement among many African leaders, businesses, and workers that are benefiting directly from this massive Chinese investment in African development.

I have personally observed this Chinese-partnered development in evidence in Ghana, Togo, Benin, and Kenya. Extensive reports exist to confirm that this is taking place not only across the African continent but in South America, Central America, the Caribbean, parts of Europe, among Islamist nations and even in parts of the U.S. The position formerly held by the U.S. as the dominating economic superpower is gradually and steadily shifting to the new partner in town. Many journalists have observed that the deals the Chinese are offering are without the political and cultural demands that were so harshly imposed by Western colonists, the IMF and World Bank as well as other lending agencies.

Thus, a significant motivator behind the scenes which I claim is driving this renewed and *heightened paranoia* about Ebola and killer African epidemics is clandestine subterfuge intended to counter and usurp China in Africa. Yet, strategies relying on fakery, covert manipulation, crises causation, and Cold War-era tactics are inevitably bound to backfire and fail in this new era of geopolitics. Just look at the failed Western machinations toward control over Middle East oil production. Those unholy wars have generated much more significant problems for the nations whose security agencies fabricated and distorted intelligence to produce the desired conflict over which they mistakenly thought they could prevail.

China is succeeding in its competition against the former colonial powers for several reasons, not the least of which is a very sizeable, literate, and disciplined workforce. For the same reasons, African countries have a high potential to rise to the heights of national productivity, sovereign wealth development, and self-determination over the coming half-century. Specific nations such as South Africa, Angola, Nigeria, Kenya, Rwanda, Ethiopia, Ghana, and others are examples wherein such positive growth in the gross domestic product (GDP) is taking place and is expected to be sustained. As with China, a spectrum of internal conditions must align to assure that this rise is ultimately sustainable toward superpower projection. Like China, these African nations can expect resistance from the U.S. and the former colonial powers that they are displacing.

Chapter 6 – A New "Scramble for Africa"

Across the African continent, we are witnessing intense competition between the old colonial powers and emerging economic powerhouses. When we speak of the former colonial powers (to include the U.S. because of its post-WWII record of hostile intervention and domination across the continent), we are primarily referring to the United Kingdom, France, Belgium, Spain, Italy, and Portugal. Notable emerging economic powers that are making a serious play for African resources are led by China and Brazil but will also include India, Russia, and South Korea. Additionally, because of a lack of arable land within their territories, many Arab states are also increasing their thrusts into African nations to feed their populations. Of course, history notes well the impact of Arab incursion into the northernmost lands of the African continent and the long account of an abominable spectrum of offenses committed against African people, their culture, and economies. Further, Israel has not been idle when it comes to manipulative and unwelcomed interference within the political, economic, and security affairs of African nations.

Looking specifically at what these foreign nations are competing for, we are alerted to the immense potential within these African regions to ultimately develop the capacity to exploit their abundant resources for industry and historic opportunities to empower themselves.

Not all foreign involvement with African countries is an obstacle to sovereign development. All great nations trade with other nations. Our challenge is to examine each of these relationships and to assure that these trade arrangements are equitable and that they allow the people within the less-developed partner nations to advance their wealth and self-determining capabilities.

The United States is currently interested in three critical areas of thrust into African regions. Their primary interest is to preserve as much as possible their great advantage in imbalanced trade across Africa since the regression of the British colonial empire after WWII. These three areas are 1) pharmaceutical drugs and healthcare supplies, 2) the energy sector, including power generating facilities, and 3) security through the U.S. Africa Command (AFRICOM). Yet, our focused examination of all three of these areas reveals severe flaws in these strategic initiatives proposed by the U.S. as they would likely introduce more risk than an advantage to African partners to such agreements. Let's examine these three areas further.

1. **Pharmaceuticals & Healthcare Supplies** – The primary hypothesis that I am putting forward as to *why* this Ebola hysteria has arisen at this time is that this pandemic is once again an American invention to *create a fear-based demand* that the U.S. supply additional medical capacity to any African nations that would accept it. As was the case with the African HIV pandemic (another concoction of the military-corporate alliance which dominates U.S. foreign policy), the plan is to make the whole of the African continent as addicted to the U.S. manufactured drugs as has become the domestic population. Over 50% of American adults are on some form of long-term pharmaceutical protocol. Achieving a similar rate of penetration into a continental African society which has now topped one billion persons and is forecast to increase to two billion before 2050, would, of course, present a long term windfall for whichever drug manufacturers could capture such a market.

This same issue came to a head during the Clinton

administration with the hostile showdown between South African President Thabo Mbeki and western drug manufacturers when Mbeki strongly resisted allowing foreign corporations to dominate S.A. pharmaceutical production even though the nation already had in place adequate drug manufacturing capacity. His government sought merely to *license* manufacturing sought-after medications, as is the practice among cooperating European and American firms. The western powers were demanding that their pharmaceutical manufacturers supply the drugs and that S.A. open up its markets to allow them to have access to the citizenry of South Africa. President Mbeki took a lot of heat for what I concluded was a correct stance and sovereign right.

With the current widespread hysteria over Ebola, it is being pressed once again that Africans will not be able to overcome their disease conditions unless they allow western corporations to enjoy free access to their rapidly increasing middle-class healthcare markets.

2. **The Energy Sector, to Include Supplying Power Generating Facilities** – As costs and risks of accessing oil from western Asia (the so-called "Middle East"), Russia, Venezuela, and other nations are becoming increasingly difficult for oil and natural gas-dependent countries, the world is increasingly turning to the African continent to fill in the widening gap in energy supplies.

In my book ***THE SUN RISES IN THE EAST: African Growth and Development for the 21st Century***, I highlighted rising productivity in oil and natural gas extraction taking place across the continent. I highlighted such energy-rich producers as Angola, Nigeria, Equatorial Guinea, the Republic of the Congo, Libya, Algeria, and South Sudan. As well were noted several new players within Africa who are rapidly developing energy production, including Ghana, Ethiopia, Kenya, Uganda, Tanzania, and Mozambique.

Beyond hydrocarbon fuels, the immense potential in other energy sectors has served as a magnet for expanding development interests from around the world. Africa has almost unlimited potential for hydroelectric power expansion, solar power, wind, wave, geothermal, and biomass energy generating capacity. One can be very assured that influence or domination over large parts of such energy capacity is among the primary motives driving a new scramble for Africa.

Much has been made of the proposed Power Africa initiative announced by President Obama during his 2013 tour of Africa. According to promises made during the trip to South Africa, Senegal and Tanzania, some $7 billion of U.S. government funding was being proposed to develop some 10,000 megawatts of "clean electricity generating capacity" within partner countries to include Ghana, Ethiopia, Kenya, Liberia, Nigeria and Tanzania, all areas where China has already committed much more substantial development initiatives.[8] A significant concern that we might have is that the contracts would go to entrenched corporations like General Electric, as was revealed in a critical article from *Forbes Magazine* which stated, in part: "General Electric will be perhaps the biggest beneficiary of that $7 billion in U.S. taxpayer funds that Obama says will underwrite Power

---

[8] GEOPOLITICAL MANEUVERING, Africa Report Vol. 5 Aug. 2013, from www.ChinaAfrica.cn

Africa...”[9]

Ultimately, bringing reliable power to 70% of Africans who currently are underserved will be the consequence of a mix of conventional, renewable, and innovative energy delivery systems. Microgrid energy systems can be supplied for as little as $100 that can bring 10 watts of solar-powered LED lighting and phone charging to one household. Other solutions within our power to implement could include systems that empower an entire village or province. Our principal concern is that in the end, African communities are empowered to educate their children to construct and maintain these systems into perpetuity.

3. **Security & the US Africa Command (AFRICOM)**– From the beginning of decades of the “Cold War” forward, America’s security policies regarding Africa have consistently undermined continental sovereignty and created a myriad of conditions through which often indescribable suffering has resulted. From supporting the despicable Apartheid regime in South Africa, overthrowing dozens of democratically elected governments, assassinating leaders, creation of “failed states,” unleashing toxic chemicals and biological agents, to vulture capitalism and cultural imperialism – the record of U.S. interventions across the continent leave us great room to doubt that this proverbial “zebra can change its stripes.”

Thus, when we see the U.S. security establishment creating a mass of hype and hysteria imagining that Islamic terrorism, Russia, China, and indigenous tribal dynamics pose such a

---

[9] Obama's 'Power Africa' Plan Greases Billions In Deals For General Electric, by Christopher Helman, Forbes online, July 1, 2013

danger to African development that the U.S. *must* bring in military assets to prevent chaos and disorder, there is plenty of reason for us to be alarmed and skeptical. Unfortunately, many African leaders have dubious records of selling out their national interests in cooperation with foreign powers.

The list of African nations collaborating with AFRICOM includes Nigeria, Djibouti, Somalia, Ethiopia, South Sudan, Uganda, Ghana, Liberia, Cote d'Ivoire, and others. In addition to AFRICOM, a spectrum of European Union member states are similarly striving to keep military assets and strategies working on the continent and within its coastal waters. Euro powers pursuing these security interventions include France, Germany, Portugal, Spain, the Netherlands, Denmark, and the United Kingdom. Other regional powers to include Arab nations, Turkey, and Brazil, have also participated in security maneuvers.[10] Despite all of these military incursions and interventions, there is conflicting evidence that overall African security is improving.

To summarize, in the context of what I have described as this "new scramble for Africa," there is indeed reason to be highly concerned. In particular, for myself and others, the integrity and exploitation of Africa's seemingly unlimited agricultural production potential is of immediate concern. If African nations follow the Western model, particularly that of the U.S., and allow multinational corporations to assume control of a predicted *tripling* of African agricultural output by 2030, then African consumers will be increasingly exposed to dangerous pesticides and other agricultural chemicals, genetically modified foods (engineered to control their natural expressions), rapidly

---

[10] AFRICOM Expands Operations and Strengthens Cooperation With Europe, by Abayomi Azikiwe, NSNBC International, Apr 22, 2014

increased prices, high amounts of stress-inducing food processing with chemical and drug additives, as well as other dangers which may not even have been revealed as of yet. One of the possible outcomes of such misdirection would be that a half-billion or more new pharmaceutical drug-dependent adults could arise over the next quarter-century from within the African continent alone.

This domination by foreign interests doesn't have to be so. Africa has the potential to develop as the unquestionable world leader in sustainable, organic food production. It will take a monumental effort on the part of a well-organized sustainability leadership cadre to guide this humongous agricultural potential into a safe, non-toxic actuality.

Chapter 7 – The Solution, Determined by the Problem

The most significant accumulation of human rights violations that humanity has ever known has been the millennium-long disruption of indigenous African societies through invasion, enslavement, the exportation of youthful and skilled labor of continental residents in both the Arab and Trans-Atlantic slave experiences, colonial conquest, massive slaughter of indigenous populations and the yet-ongoing racist oppression of black-skinned communities of virtually every nation on the planet.

We can witness even to current times that nations continue to organize for warfare, killing of fellow-humans, inhumane exploitation, to ignore immense suffering, and starvation among the world's most innocent populations. Humans can love and hate one another to Life and Death; too often, it seems as if there is a fragile line between these extremes of human sentiment toward their fellow humans.

Yet, within the context of this terrible and ongoing history, we still awaken each day with a spirit rising within our hearts to do better today; to somehow engage a new paradigm shift that will uplift humanity and guide us further toward our most noble ideals. The ancients called it the *Summum Bonum*, which translates to "The Greatest Good." With such a durable and highly moral valuation as driving motivation, one can see opportunity all around to sow the seeds of a better outcome and to help create a world in which we can each express our highest potential.

With such a guiding foundation, even though there is so much chaos and avarice being expressed in the world we are witnessing, we can nonetheless tune in to the Voice of Truth speaking from within the depths of every human. Peacemakers perceive another pathway amid hatred and hostility. Real progressives turn every challenge into a means by which the most humane ideals are advanced. Creative and resourceful people look for problems and challenges all around them to have the opportunity to confirm their belief in our collective creativity and resourcefulness.

I write as one of those who are convinced that there are *no problems* that are affecting the African continent, along with its Diaspora communities that are insurmountable. From such a perspective, the statement that "the solution is in the problem" should make so much sense as it challenges us to dip deep into our natural resourcefulness and creativity, to think outside the box, and to propose magnificent changes to existing habits and toward doing things differently.

The great paradox before us is how current leaders of African nations, organizations, and agencies don't do a better job of guiding our immense collective resources toward better outcomes and resolution of long-term grievances and problems. Yet, a significant component of such problem solving is an accurate analysis of the conditions within which a problem is being presented. There is just no escaping the fact that a part of "human nature" is exploitive, selfish to the point of becoming damaging, and prone to wish upon one's own "genetic nationality" benefits that are not to be equally shared with those regarded as outsiders. As such, people naturally organize into groups, work in earnest to instill identity, and a sense of pride among other members of their self-determined group, along with their children, and construct pathways toward empowerment for the group. Members of viable groups are taught that they have value and that it is worth self-sacrifice upon the part of each member of the group to preserve group integrity, sovereignty, and sustainability.

Then we come to examine unhealthy groups who, too often, seem to only come together as a reaction to some real or imagined hurt to themselves and other members with which they associate themselves. Disconcertingly, members of unhealthy groups might pride themselves upon pain and deprivation as sort of a "badge of identification" and grounds for rallying their members to collectivize. Too often, this has been the case among Afri-Amers who spend an excessive amount of often limited resources rallying against oppression while overlooking opportunities to create the type of institutional transformation which would mitigate the impact of a steady stream of such offenses.

Within such context, "racism" could be considered either (or both) a motivating advantage or a crippling plague. We can see distinction explained within the pages of Joel Kotkin's revealing book, ***TRIBES: How Race, Religion and Identity Determine Success in the New Global Economy***. In the hands of an empowered class, racial alignment is yet another tool to advance the likelihood that their ethnic group will empower their children and future generations. From the standpoint of a victim, racism is an obstacle difficult to overcome even across generations. This presents a paradox. Either there are multiple expressions of the same racism theory, or there is something greater operating within the *culture* of different ethnic groups, which either leads toward empowerment or disempowerment. I suggest that this paradox forces us to conclude that "the solution is in the problem."

There has always risen within every generation a forward-thinking type of new leadership that sees opportunity in abundance. They can reasonably assess resources available at any given time to their group as well as rivals. These individuals seize every chance to adapt, draw upon available skills and creativity, and to envision how small and large changes in habitual patterns can redirect themselves and their followers toward a better outcome. We return to the often-quoted idea from Albert Einstein (himself one of history's most notable *outside-the-box thinkers*), "Insanity is doing the same thing over and over and expecting different results." Thus we seek out an alternative pathway and move to the beat of a different drummer.

Chapter 8 – The World Bank and IMF

Some argue that capitalism has spawned the root of most of the contemporary evils of the world. Why do we continue to witness so much war, hatred, violence, greed, exploitation, and avarice? Why does the super-rich hoard so much while masses of the poor suffer despite the nearly unlimited abundance of this precious gem of a planet? Can we figure out *what in the hell* is going on here?

If one were to ask me, the guiltiest culprits are the money lenders and speculators. They have set up a massive scheme to steal away our essential humanity. Thousands of years ago, a conspiracy among the wealthy arose within the world that schemed to control as much as possible while working the absolute least that they could get away with. Their plot was to control the fruits of the labor of others by usury schemes.

Money is commonly referred to as "currency," which also analogous to the same "current" that is the flow of electricity; energy in motion. While we could go into an extensive discourse on the U.S. Federal Reserve System (the most complex and advanced usury system developed to date), I'll condense it to a few simple ideas:

1. Usury is an unrighteous scheme by which a capitalist oligarch has set up a system to suppress our innate tendency to produce for self and those within our sphere of mutual identification;

2. The dominance of moneylenders within nations has always been linked to warfare and the opportunistic exploitation of national disasters;

3. After private bankers selfishly exploit national assets, working populations and the public coffers begin to suffer the consequences as national resources are redirected more and more into private wealth. This downward national economic cycle persists until the need for yet another war arises, and the exploitation cycle can reset itself;

4. The path by which the U.S. came to dominate the globe in the aftermath of the second great European war was based mainly on militarism, money lending and violently dominating the world's petroleum supplies along with other strategic resources;

5. The worst thing that can happen to national unity is the concentration of wealth and income. This is *the* major challenge within the U.S. and the larger world today.

After WWII, 744 delegates from America and the Allied powers gathered together at Breton Woods, New Hampshire, in July 1944. The conference was known as the *United Nations Monetary and Financial Conference,* and it was the largest capitalist scheme ever devised to date. While a large part of their plan involved the creation of the *International Bank for Reconstruction and Development*, to finance the reconstruction of a devastated Europe and Asia, their lasting legacy has been the system through which developing nations outside of the original conference planners have been financially exploited, their resources scooped up in unfair exchange, and the massive disruption to the course of countries around the globe. Africa, Latin America, South Asia, and the more impoverished regions have been the worst affected by the Breton Woods usury and governance schemes.

The two major institutions which have persisted from this unholy gathering of the wealthy have been the *World Bank* and the *International Monetary Fund*. Herein I provide a brief description of each:

The World Bank

In brief, the Wikipedia description of the World Bank says:

> "The World Bank is a United States international economical institution that provides social aids to developing countries for capital programs. The World Bank is a division of the World Bank Group, and a member of the United Nations Development Group."

The institution was created in the aftermath of the Second World War and was intended to reconstruct war-destroyed Europe with France receiving the first loan. One thing particular about the World Bank is that it has always made strict demands for political and economic reform as a condition for receiving its assistance. Thus before granting funds to the French for rebuilding their national infrastructure,

> "...the United States State Department told the French government that its members associated with the Communist Party would first have to be removed. The French government complied with this diktat and removed the Communist coalition government. Within hours, the loan to France was approved." [11]

To this date, one of the primary criticisms of the World Bank is that it is too politically demanding and has been used as an instrument to bolster capitalist nation exploitation of needs

---

[11] World Bank, from Wikipedia, the free encyclopedia /
http://en.wikipedia.org/wiki/World_Bank#1944.E2.80.931968

within developing countries. Three principle criticisms of the institution include:

1. **Structural Adjustment** – loans that are tied to political, social, and governing changes, which include privatization of national assets. Structural Adjustment Programs (SAPs) become harsher as nations, for a variety of reasons, find it difficult to repay loans and interest. These painful changes to a nation's economy have triggered much domestic upheaval within affected countries.

2. **Fairness of Assistance Conditions** – Many critics have condemned how wealthy lending nations demand severe changes within more unfortunate borrowers, which affect portions of the population most vulnerable and in need of government assistance.

3. **Sovereign Immunity** – The World Bank demands that it remains immune from any consequence which takes place within the borrower nation because of actions that it has required to fulfill its lending requirements. These actions have even included forcing school fees on low-income families, forcing privatization of a state-owned telecom as a condition for receiving hurricane aid, and eliminating food subsidies in post-invasion Iraq. [12]

International Monetary Fund

The IMF was created at the Bretton Woods Conference in 1944 with the contribution of 29 member countries. Its stated mission was to develop a means by which international payments could be facilitated. Under their plan, nations with trade imbalances could borrow from the pool to further trade. Today the

---

[12] The World Bank as the Perfect Standard Bearer, Klein, Naomi (27 April 2007) The Guardian / cited in Wikipedia

organization describes itself as an "organization of 188 countries, working to foster global monetary cooperation, secure financial stability, facilitate international trade, promote high employment and sustainable economic growth, and reduce poverty around the world." [13]

Despite such noble stated intentions, the International Monetary Fund stands as one of the most intrusive, despised, and manipulative international agencies of the modern era. According to research from the Overseas Development Institute, the IMF supports what one activist called "global apartheid." The ODI report listed five main criticisms of the IMF as such:

1. It is a racist, capitalist manipulator of developing nations' ambitions.

2. The IMF blames the victims for economic problems that are primarily caused by wealthier nations' trade and finance policies and has even gone so far as to suppress access to food within debt-challenged countries.

3. The final consequence of IMF policies is often actually degrading national development and employment within borrower nations, with the poorest being the worst affected.

4. That IMF "medicine" was often self-defeating and frequently made matters far worse, thus deepening the cycle of dependency, debt, and default.

5. That IMF policies were inconsistent and irrational, being delivered ad hoc across the spectrum of nations, frequently reflecting governments who were friend or foe during political currents. The IMF has long been accused of support of military dictatorships friendly to Anglo-American and

---

[13] International Monetary Fund, from Wikipedia, the free encyclopedia / http://en.wikipedia.org/wiki/International_Monetary_Fund

European corporations, thus making the financial group *anti-democracy* in its working policies.

Even former U.S. president Bill Clinton has voiced harsh words about his role in using IMF structural adjustment programs against developing nations:

> "We need the World Bank, the IMF, all the big foundations, and all the governments to admit that, for 30 years, we all blew it, including me when I was president. We were wrong to believe that food was like some other product in international trade, and we all have to go back to a more responsible and sustainable form of agriculture." [14]

For the prospering, sustainable Africa that we envision as a hallmark of civilization for the next millennium, our global presence demands autonomous and sovereign economic foundations. We are thus challenged to move beyond the neo-imperialist policies of the IMF, World Bank, other Bretton Woods organizations, as well as pressured influence from Washington, London, Geneva, and Paris over African security, economic, environmental, and human rights affairs.

Africans from across the globe have amassed a vast spectrum of skills and resources. We can build a truly spectacular "Great Swahili Empire," which can last for thousands of years into the future. Ultimately, we will require partners outside of our ethnicity with which to build this destiny. We certainly must engage more equitable partnerships toward this purpose.

---

[14] Former U.S. president Bill Clinton, Speech at United Nations World Food Day, October 16, 2008

Chapter 9 – The BRICS Development Partners

One of the most dramatic challenges to arise to the hegemony of the World Bank, IMF, and western banking hierarchy is the new wealth of China and Brazil combined with the technical and resource wealth of Russia, India, and South Africa. This collective has come to be known in geopolitical circles by the acronym *BRICS (Brazil, Russia, India, China, and South Africa).* There can be no denying that BRICS has rapidly risen to be the most competitive force in the world today to unseat the western powers that have dominated global affairs for the past 500 years.

In this chapter, I detail some of the areas through which BRICS nations have attained greater influence over global affairs.

China

China's industrial capacity has exceeded that of all other countries, including the U.S., coming to dominate consumer goods manufacturing, steel production, leading the world in gross agricultural production. As well, China is now the world leader in the total value of industrial output, mining, and ore processing. China is the world's leading exporting nation and has the largest money reserves. The *CIA World Factbook* has the following to share regarding China's industry:

"Industries: the world leader in gross value of industrial output; mining and ore processing, iron, steel, aluminum, and other metals; coal; machine building; armaments; textiles and apparel; petroleum; cement; chemicals; fertilizers; consumer products (including footwear, toys, and electronics); food processing; transportation equipment, including automobiles, rail cars and locomotives, ships, aircraft; telecommunications equipment, commercial space launch vehicles, satellites." [15]

Additionally, China's high rate of Foreign Direct Investment (FDI) in developing nation economies is one of the significant geopolitical phenomena transforming the world today. Across the African continent in 2013, China's investments totaled about 40.7 billion dollars, yielding a return in trade partnerships of about five dollars to each one invested. Their African investments are quite diverse and include mining, oil extraction, food processing, telecommunications, transportation, construction, power generation, waste disposal, seaport development, automobile manufacturing, banking services, and even shoe manufacturing. [16]

Brazil

Brazil is South America's largest and most populous nation. It has become the dominant economic power in South and Central America as well as much of the Caribbean. Since the end of a U.S.-backed military dictatorship in 1985, the country's gross development has been quite a spectacular phenomenon. Much of Brazil's wealth is in natural resources, commodities, industrial production, and export, including automobiles, airplanes, other transport equipment, iron ore, soybeans, coffee along with many other resource-based products.

Brazil's financial strength as the eighth highest in GDP purchasing power parity (PPP) in the world has now come to exert itself

---

[15] The World Factbook: China, 2014, www.CIA.gov
[16] Separating Fact from Fiction in the China-Africa Relationship, from www.PsC.com

throughout South America as well as the Caribbean. Brazil's level of foreign direct investment (FDI) has come to rival that of the U.S. with specific projects such as a nearly $1 billion development assistance grant to Cuba to expand the Mariel Seaport on Cuba's south coast. The Brazil-Cuba investment created the most modern seaport serving the Caribbean, Central and South America. Similar investments in South America and Africa totaled nearly $180 billion in 2013. Foreign investment in Brazil's strong domestic economy has risen to exceed an annual $663 billion, according to the CIA World Factbook. China has surpassed the U.S. as Brazil's leading import and export partner. [17]

Russia

Russia has long stood as a symbol of defiance to European and American ambitions despite an extensive record of striving to accommodate friendship and cooperation with the West. There are many facts about Russia that escape the attention of Americans. These facts need comprehension to see that its role as a significant player in global economics for the foreseeable future is not to be ignored. Russia is one of the oldest nations on earth, founded in the 12th Century and is the single largest country on Earth in terms of geographic space. Despite a continuous chain of domestic political and economic upheavals during the 20th Century, Russia emerged with a significant modernized industry, a leading high-tech sector, significant agricultural production, extensive mining, auto manufacturing, heavy industries including shipbuilding, a very high respectable balance with resultant high currency and gold reserves. As well, Russia has amongst the world's highest levels of both petroleum and natural gas production. The Russian nation enjoys one of the

---

[17] The World Factbook: Brazil, 2014, www.CIA.gov

lowest rates of public debt in the world today, with only about a tenth of the public debt of the U.S.[18]

Currently, because of Russia's opposition to the march of "green revolutions" around the world (which are covertly sponsored by Western intelligence agencies), America and certain European Union countries are attempting to reign in Russia with a set of economic sanctions and oil production strategies which are aimed at cutting back Russia's development capital. These reactionary and ill-thought policies are in very great danger of backfiring, and there is already complaining from EU nations that support of the sanctions hurts current, and future markets as Russia then turns to China and other southern hemisphere nations to replace what they had been getting from EU states.

It is the level of economic cooperation between Russia and China that stirs the most significant level of fear within its competitors, America, Great Britain, and the European Union. Sanctions have only served to speed up the rate at which Russia was turning eastward and creating a spectrum of pacts with China which have raised their alliance, along with the cooperation of other BRICS countries and many developing nations, to be the undeniable dominant economic block for the remainder of the 21st Century and beyond. The Chinese news service *Xinhuanet* very recently has the following to say on many of these new developments between Russia and China:

> SOCHI, Russia, Oct. 11 (Xinhua) – Economic cooperation between China and Russia is long-term, stable and sustainable, which serves both countries' interests and benefits world economy, visiting Chinese Vice Premier Wang Yang said Saturday.

---

[18] CIA World Factbook: Russia /
https://www.cia.gov/library/publications/the-world-factbook/geos/rs.html

> China is willing to export to Russia more products such as oil-and-gas related items, communication equipment, industrial consumer and agricultural goods, Wang said at a meeting with Russian Deputy Prime Minister Dmitry Rogozin.

> Also, China eyes more imports of Russia's electromechanical and high-tech products, adding both sides should spare unremitting efforts to raise their trade volume to 100 billion U.S. dollars in 2015.

During the meeting, Chinese and Russian officials hailed cooperation in such strategic spheres as long-range wide-body aircraft development, nuclear power utilization, satellite navigation systems development, and aerospace programs.

According to analysis from many knowledgeable sources, the alliance between Russia and China which utilizes Russia's vast natural resource and military capacity, combined with Chinese industry and export-derived cash reserves, is the dominant relationship in the world today which is driving a "global reset" in economic hegemony, al with a political and strategic transformation from a Europe-dominant world sphere to one in which Asian and southern hemisphere nations dominate; thus this ushers into a close of the 500-year cycle of the *Age of Mercantilism*, whereby European and American capitalism dictated the affairs of nearly the entire population of the globe.

India

India is another significant player not only because of its inclusion within BRICS but also due to the rate of development of industry and international trade. Like China, the European Union, and Sub-Saharan Africa, India's large population and *demographic advantage* have driven demand for domestic consumption of its natural resources and direction of government policies to serve such a large population. Modern India only emerges after the end of British colonial domination in the mid-20th Century. It was India's emergence as a nuclear power in 1998 that accompanied its ascension as a modern, industrialized nation worthy of respect from countries that had once ruthlessly exploited its population.

While India is undoubtedly burdened by its legacy of wealth concentration, racism, and caste hierarchy, its successful development of a high-tech sector, educated workforce, market economic policies, healthcare, information communications technologies (ICT) and industrial manufacturing have all served to make India the 4th largest economy in the world today behind the U.S., EU, and China, just ahead of Japan and Germany. Continuing wealth disparity within India is still problematic, undoubtedly a legacy of the caste hierarchy. Still, the nation has managed to expand a vast set of agricultural products, petroleum products, precious gemstones, metal industries, chemical production, apparel, and automobile manufacturing, also to include a robust and growing healthcare tourism economy. [19]

Additionally, like China, India has become a significant trading partner and FDI investor across the African continent. Having gained much of a cultural foothold within Africa during the age of British colonial domination, today, many Indians are returning to exploit a spectrum of business opportunities. There is great concern that Indian merchants do not exhibit the type of social values that are conducive to Africa's long-term self-interest. Nonetheless, it is increasingly common to see the high level of Indian participation within African economies, especially in the eastern and southern portions of the continent.

---

[19] CIA World Factbook: India / www.CIA.gov

South Africa

South Africa is the only African nation to be officially included in the BRICS strategic planning, even though more than two dozen other countries have been vying for BRICS membership or inclusive partnership. Like so many other African nations, South Africa is technically a creation of Dutch and English colonial settlers who carved out the colony from several indigenous African kingdoms. Thus, traditional non-cohesiveness of the native peoples facilitated the takeover and dominance by these racist settlers from 1652 until the birth of the post-apartheid state in 1994. The vile and despised apartheid government, which dominated Southern Africa with the assistance of the Anglo-American powers, created an industrial, military, and science-based nation to serve their and their backers' self-interest. Now that this state is in the hands of an elected government, it is sometimes difficult to accept that such a vast segment of the economy is still dominated by the very institutions which created and sustained the brutal apartheid era.

South Africa (called Azania by many natives and Pan Africans) is blessed with a bounty of natural resources rivaling any nation on Earth to include a spectrum of minerals, precious gemstones, rare earth substances, industrial metals, and natural gas. It has a substantial agricultural base yet has developed only about 3.4% of its arable land. Similarly, with renewable water resources, it currently utilizes less than 25% of water available on an annual basis. While periodic droughts continue to plague parts of South Africa, modern industrial, energy and agricultural development show promise for the nation to continue to enjoy tremendous growth in agricultural output.

South Africa is undeniably the driving industrial base of the SADC region (Southern Africa Development Commission), leading the world in producing platinum, gold, and chromium, among many mined commodities. Heavy industry thrives in the nation as well as manufacturing automobiles, metalworking, machinery, textiles, steel, chemicals, processed foods, and ship repair. [20] Despite an unemployment rate of nearly a quarter of the population, its labor force of 18.5 million is among the most considerable underdeveloped resources on Earth. Wealth inequality, a powerful legacy of the apartheid era, is still a terrible problem in South Africa. The nation's leading import and export partner is China, with the U.S. the second leading importer of raw materials. Imports from China, Germany, Saudi Arabia, U.S., Japan, and India consist of machinery and equipment, chemicals, petroleum products, scientific instruments, and processed foodstuffs, according to the *CIA World Factbook* for 2014.

Many believe that South Africa is the key to the liberation of the determined economic potential of the entire Southern Region of Africa. As the dominating partner in the prospering SADC region, its influence over neighboring countries is indisputable. Still, South Africa's acquiescence to western security policies such as tolerating the invasion and destruction of the Libyan state, along with the gross disparity of wealth within the nation, indicates that South Africa's black majority governance has a degree of maturation yet ahead for it to finally assume its rightful place among the wealthy and powerful nations of the Earth.

Future Collaboration

We can only speculate as to what the future holds. As William Clay is famously quoted, "This is quite a game, politics. There are no permanent enemies, and no permanent friends, only permanent interests." With 55 nations on the continent and more than 22 majority-black countries around the globe, it is a great time for Africans to pursue sovereign development.

---

[20] CIA World Factbook: South Africa, 2014 / www.CIA.gov

Chapter 10 – Great Opportunities in A New Africa

There are just so many opportunities that have risen to viability within the context of 55 African nations moving from poverty, war, and exploitation into newly emergent economic status, that it would take a much larger book to attempt to cover them all. Nonetheless, individuals need to be aware of these investment and industrial development trends so that we can become more significant players in this **New Scramble for Africa**. Constant study and tuning into business and financial news from around the globe is highly recommended, as you will undoubtedly observe that this is a rapidly transforming climate.

We will point out just a few of the more significant growth areas, each of which could be further subdivided into a much broader spectrum of areas for expansion.

Automobile Manufacturing

I awaken most days intending to discover something exciting and new with which to share with my committed Pan African associates. On one particular day, a brilliant research associate shared via the social network a particularly exciting news release from *Business Daily Africa* about a new, low-cost Kenya-manufactured all-terrain motor vehicle called the Mobius II, which is being marketed for only Sh950,000 Kenya Shillings, or $10,626 US dollars.[21] The all-terrain vehicle is being assembled by the accomplished Kenya corporation Kenya Vehicle Manufacturers. KVM has an extensive line of motor vehicles,

---

[21] Low Cost Kenya Made Car Goes on Sale at Sh950,000, from the Business Daily online edition, www.BusinessDailyAfrica.com

including luxury buses, SUVs, safari trucks, long-haul trailers, campers, and other products. [22]

Additionally, we are excited about similar developments in motor vehicle manufacturing taking place in Nigeria through the Innoson Vehicle Manufacturing Company, which produces SUVs, buses, dump trucks, pickup trucks, motorcycles, and, more recently, a sedan.

Ghana has the seeds of an impressive motor vehicle industry, and one particular family, that of Apostle Dr. Kwadwo Safo owners of the Kantanka Group of Companies, is displaying the most brilliant genius in engineering that the continent has perhaps ever witnessed. This father-and-son led effort is producing a spectrum of manufactured products from autos to a self-designed helicopter. Here's just a portion of what Al-Jazeera had to say about this unbelievable set of accomplishments:

> Accra, Ghana - Imagine having a television set that comes on after an effortless clap or by blowing air; picture yourself in a car that is engineless and starts with a simple push of a button tucked to your dress; or a change-over-machine that speaks and tells you where exactly a fire or electrical fault is in your home.

> This is not fiction. It is not magic. It is not happening in Europe or Asia and not even in the United States. These products are being manufactured in the West African nation of Ghana.

> The brains behind this is Apostle Dr. Kwadwo Safo, owner of the Kantanka Group of Companies. He is naturally gifted. A genius. An inventor and a philanthropist. He has no formal or sophisticated technical background. He

---

[22] Kenya Vehicle Manufacturers website / www.KVM.co.ke

imagines, dreams and creates at will. He lives in his own world. [23]

Additionally, I must point out the exciting work being done at Uganda's Makerere University (the MIT of East Africa), which has a broad spectrum of research projects, including a completed electric vehicle, the Kiira EV. According to the university website, "The strategic goal of the vehicle design project is to incubate a Centre for Research in transportation technologies with a vision of presenting a wholesome solution to the transportation needs in Uganda."[24] Their work is shockingly brilliant!

While South Africa assembles a lot of motor vehicles for domestic sale and export, these are all the products of multinational corporations using the nation for assembly and sourcing.

> "The automotive and components industry is well placed for investment opportunities. Vehicle manufacturers such as BMW, Ford (incorporating Mazda), General Motors, Mercedes Benz, Nissan, Renault, Toyota and Volkswagen have production plants in South Africa, while component manufacturers such as Arvin Exhaust, Bloxwich, Corning, Senior Flexonics have established production bases here." [25]

Agriculture

For so many reasons, developing agricultural industries across the African continent is one of the most significant opportunities presented in centuries. Numerous media and financial institutions, including the United Nations and World Bank

---

[23] Ghana's Talented but Ignored Inventors, from AlJazeera.com news,

[24] The Kiira EV, from the website of the College of Engineering, Design, Art and Technology, Makerere University, Kampala Uganda / www.CEDAT.mak.ac.ug

[25] South Africa's Automotive Industry, from South Africa Info /

agencies, have all assessed that Africa will undergo a tremendous transformation in agricultural output within the next one to two decades. It is being projected that African agriculture will triple its annual production to reach $1 trillion by 2030. We are already witnessing much of this growth as well as a "mad scramble" by multinational agriculture interests to position themselves at the top of an expansive funnel that will supply $660 billion *new dollars* annually to African continental agriculture output.

As the population of the continent is expected to double by 2050, and that combines with the world's fastest rise in middle-class income status, the need to feed 2 billion Africans looms large. As well, because of large-scale rejection of American agricultural exports within the European Union, which is wary of GMO foods, agricultural chemicals, and compromised standards of food safety in the U.S., a question arises as to which nations will step up to fill the gap left from the rejection of U.S. agriculture products; Africans stand to be prime beneficiaries of this change.

Another danger to African production, which came to light in Zimbabwe recently, is the illegal importation of meat products from nations with government-subsidized agricultural development. The prices of chickens produced in Brazil that were illegally being imported into Zimbabwe by the family of the Vice President Joice Mujuru was condemned by the Minister of Finance and Economic Development Patrick Chinamasa after the Ministry of Agriculture issued a permit at VP Mujuru's direction. Chinamasa stated that "the decision to issue the permit amounted to shooting 'ourselves in the foot.'" [26] The Zimbabwe government judges that such subterfuge against the indigenous poultry farmers who cannot compete against cheap wholesale importation of frozen chickens, thus a threat that would justify

---

[26] Mujuru in Chicken Import Scandal, Nov. 10, 2014, Newsdze Zimbabwe /

the return of the ousted white-dominated agriculture production which has been overcome in recent decades.

African nations are significantly underutilizing their agricultural potential with just a tiny percentage of arable land and renewable water in current production. As well, there are key infrastructure developments taking place in transportation, rural manufacturing, cold storage, food processing, and water management that will further assist African-based companies in cashing in on this new food windfall.

Beyond feeding Africans and a large segment of the world outside of the continent, the demand for renewable energy is feeding demand for increased agricultural products that can be converted into biofuel. It would overwhelm this document for me to list all of the various agricultural products which will make up this new, vastly expanded African agrarian scene. It does go to say that they will include foodstuffs, culinary *and* healing herbs, biofuels, processed local products along with agriculture industry components. Should any African region commit to producing industrial hemp products, they could become the world leader in the ultimate renewable natural resource.

The October 2014 issue of *National Geographic Magazine* featured an extensive article entitled "The Next Green Revolution," written by Tim Folger. This was a very revealing report which compared the contemporary science-based revolution in global agricultural expansion to the earlier *Green Revolution* that occurred in the aftermath of WWII that depended on the introduction of a range of farming chemistry along with technology for a significant increase in food production. While the current article seemed (in my opinion) to be more of a promotion for genetic engineering corporations, it did weigh some of the severe questions about GMO crops that have made the process so controversial. [27]

One of the more exciting and inspiring components of Folger's extensive article was revealing that the East African nation of Tanzania has achieved the fourth-largest number of registered organic farms among all countries around the world. This phenomenal accomplishment is due in no small part to the efforts of one brilliant young visionary by the name of Janet Fares Maro and the organization she founded called *Sustainable Agriculture Tanzania.*   Another blog from Biovision featured an interview with Janet Maro that included the following response to a question regarding organic farming in Tanzania:

> Tanzania has about 85,000 hectares for large scale and small scale certified organic farms. About 100,000 farmers are contracted by companies to produce organic products for export. There are about 36 companies and cooperatives which are certified to export organic products. Research on benefits of organic agriculture ecologically, socially and economically is still on-going. In Tanzania organic farming is mostly confused by traditional farming in which no inputs are used and therefore on this basis one can say that many small scale farms are organic by default. When it comes to certified organic farming, there are very few certified large scale organic farms which mostly produce coffee, cotton, cocoa, spices like lemongrass and paprika, tea and fruits. Tanzania is still behind as compared to neighbors Kenya and Uganda, the few organic products here are mostly for export. [28]

---

[27] The Next Green Revolution, by Tim Folger, National Geographic Magazine, October 2014

[28] Interview of the Week 46: Janet Maro, Agronomist and Expert for Organic Agriculture from Tanzania, Biovision Blog, November 16, 2011

My final point on this topic relates to an outstanding and open-ended invitation extended by leaders of African nations for experienced farmers from Diaspora countries to return and become a part of this new global ascendance in agricultural production. I've had multiple encounters with such leadership from 2006 when, in Cairo, Egypt, the Zimbabwe ambassador to Egypt and the then-governor of the Harare district (capital of Zimbabwe) asked me to join them for dinner to discuss the participation of experienced Afri-Amer farmers in the restructuring of that nation's farming sector. Thus I can testify beyond all doubt that our experiences in building the base for America's agricultural economic supremacy will serve us well to construct an even greater set of future partnerships not only in Zimbabwe but across the African continent.

Repatriating farmers are being offered free land, access to top levels of government, and university assistance along with premier positioning within contracts that are being extended to encourage agricultural partnerships with local small-scale producers. There is just no question that the opportunity to make phenomenal wealth is being extended within this new African agrarian expansion. To ignore such golden opportunity becomes unthinkable once one has acquired and fully comprehended these facts.

I contend that U.S. and Diaspora-based agricultural experts and producers have a vital role to play in maintaining the integrity of this anticipated tripling of African agriculture that is being forecast for the coming decade and more. Key factors toward this growth include:

a. Tapping African nations' rapidly expanding middle-class consumers for our products;

b.   Providing export for modern farm equipment, harvesters, and irrigation systems;

c.   Training a new generation of U.S.-based farming professionals as well as extending this training to African partners;

d.   Transferring our agricultural technology professionals to the continent in large numbers;

e.   Providing safe seed stocks, organic farming supplies, and eco-friendly farming expertise to Africa.

f.   Supplying technology for storing, transporting, and producing finished food products to be processed close to areas of rural farm production.

g.   Diaspora Africans must also assist our continental family in protecting their domestic markets from unfair competition from (foreign) government-subsidized food imports as well as food stocks contaminated with chemicals, pesticides, and genetically engineered components.

Energy

We had earlier discussed the U.S. sponsored Power Africa Initiative in relative detail. Beyond that particular proposal, we need to look closely at the opportunities and the challenges that need to be overcome to manifest this significant infrastructure development. African nations are not "beggars at a feast" when it comes to technological innovation and economic growth. To the contrary, many of these nations are led by a highly-educated leadership cadre who have been students at some of the finest universities on the planet. As well, some of these nations have advanced to secondary and tertiary stages of industrial development and thus are well-positioned to be able to implement technical innovations that are a part of a new sustainable global economy.

Concerning African nations' collaboration with the Power Africa Initiative, there are reservations and doubts which are beginning to become more apparent. Hesitance on the part of both sides of such partnerships is being reported, and some are expressing doubt that western nations can overcome their "colonizing mentality" sufficiently enough to be able to execute such ambitious efforts. As well, the presence of Asian partners as potential competitors in this and other fields leaves these African nations in the position that the deal is going to have to be acceptable in the context of the new global economic order.

The Nigerian *National Journal* had the following to report on some of the challenges to smooth implementation of the Power Africa Initiative as related by The Minister of Power, Chinedu Nebo:

> "Whereas most of the big financial interventions in the sector have come from Asia, America and Europe have shown some form of foot-dragging in fully engaging the programme in terms of investment, a situation which must change for them to benefit from the dividends of a full-grown electricity market," the Minister intensified. [29]

And concerning the capacity and the general level of interest of his country to develop non-hydrocarbon energy sources, Minister Nebo had this to share:

---

[29] Capacity building critical to Power Africa Initiative – Chinedu Nebo, ISSUED BY, Government of the Federal Republic of Nigeria, November 3, 2014 / http://www.NationalJournal.com

> "Nigeria has enjoyed far greater solar potentials than Germany, where a great percentage of its power needs come through the sun. This source alone accounts for three times more than all other energy sources put together in the country."

For Sub-Saharan Africa to reach its full development capacity, sufficient energy must be in place to power rapidly-expanding industrial production. This needed investment is vast. Recalling our report that China invested some $40.7 billion across the continent in 2013 and reaped nearly a 5-to-1 return on its investment in trade advantage, then a proposal of as much as $3 trillion in new energy infrastructure in the coming decades might be expected to yield similar return. On October 22, 2014, *Petroleum Economist* had the following to say about this critical and timely investment:

> Sub-Saharan Africa will need $3 trillion of investment in new energy infrastructure by 2030 if the region is to raise hundreds of millions out of poverty and sustain economic growth, a new report by the International Energy Agency (IEA) said. In the IEA's Africa Energy Outlook published on 13 October, the agency said spending on energy and infrastructure in sub-Saharan Africa would need to be doubled to $110 billion per year to give millions of Africans access to affordable electricity. [30]

There are many critical challenges across Africa regarding reliable energy for the majority of the continent's inhabitants. While the scope of this section of this report must be kept brief, there are several vital points which must be made (the following facts are from Wikipedia) [31]:

---

[30] Energy Access Key to Africa's Economic Growth, by Helen Robertson, Petroleum Economist Magazine, Oct. 22, 2014

[31] Energy in Africa, from Wikipedia, the free encyclopedia, www.Wikipedia.com

- Energy is a scarce commodity across Africa compared to the developed world. The Sub-Saharan per-capita consumption in one year equates to per-capita usage in the U.S. of only 25 days.

- Electrical provisioning in the region is primarily relegated only to the urban, wealthy, and upper-middle class. At the same time, rural populations in nations such as Malawi, Ethiopia, Niger, and Chad have only 2% access.

- "Africa has an average electrification rate of 24%, while the rate in the rest of the developing world lies closer to 40%."

- A combination of irregular power supplies and underdeveloped transportation "have stunted the growth of domestic companies and discouraged foreign firms from setting up manufacturing plants" across the continent. [Quotes are from the Wiki article.]

But, all is not doom and gloom. There are spectrums of initiatives from a broad coalition of partnerships that are serving to overcome these infrastructure deficits. I covered these bright possibilities in my recent Conscious Rasta Report *The Sun Rises in the East: African Growth and Development for the 21st Century,* part of which I must repeat:

Much has been said about oil and gas resource development across Africa. The top ten oil producing countries in Africa in 2014 are (in order of production): Nigeria, Algeria, Angola, Libya, Egypt, Sudan, Equatorial Guinea, Rep. of the Congo, Gabon and South Africa. New players in this game include Ghana, Ethiopia, Kenya, Uganda, Tanzania and Mozambique. Further developments are similarly established and expanding in natural gas within these nations.

As stated before, hydroelectric power expansion across the continent is tremendous and expected to continue growing at a rapid rate. Within current capacity African nations are producing 20,300 GWh/year (gigawatts per year) in hydroelectric power. At current technological feasibility this could be expanded 86-fold to 1.75 million GWh/year with a theoretical potential continent-wide of 4 million GWh/year, an increase of nearly 200-fold.

The solar power generation potential of the continent is nearly infinite with nations such as South Africa, Algeria, Rwanda, Kenya, Gambia, Sierra Leone and others leading the charge to implement various solar strategies. Further, wind, wave, geothermal and biomass are all being explored as sustainable sources for Africa's future energy needs. [32]

Within the context of this anticipated energy expansion, there is tremendous ground for the small to the middle-sized player. Innovative technologies are being called for from non-hydrocarbon based transportation to small scale hydroelectric generators. Ocean wave technology is another exciting frontier from which Africa, with its expansive coastline, could become a world leader. As well, with the vast expanse of sun-drenched real estate, solar power has virtually unlimited potential in Africa and would be an ideal technology to access remote areas where stringing power lines would prove to be an expensive endeavor. I would strive to convince the reader that the opportunities to unleash the full development potential of the African continent

---

[32] The Sun Rises in the East: African Growth and Development for the 21st Century, The Conscious Rasta Report by Keidi Awadu, February 2014

by bringing reliable energy to all of its residents are available to each of us who are creative, resourceful, and committed to making a positive change toward an African destiny.

Tourism

No one in the modern world can escape the documentation of Africa's vast beauty, teeming wildlife, lush rainforests, and spectacular geography. Africa has everything which one could consider as beautiful and attractive. Despite the excess of media stories to the contrary, each year, tens of millions of tourists travel all parts of the continent to savor this spectacle of natural environments and to engage in the pleasures of sights, sounds, tastes, and experiences of African tourism. Within this vast stream of annual tourism, there are many great opportunities. As the middle class of the continent continues to expand at the highest rate in the world, tourism, travel and accommodations will serve as a solid base for investment, development, and innovation.

There is a broad spectrum of tourist opportunities being developed across the continent. I'll highlight just a few.

- With the rapid rise of wealth and upper-middle-class status, some entrepreneurs are introducing golf resorts to serve this growing population as well as international tourists. In Kenya, one group of investors teamed up to turn a former sisal plantation into a projected 2500 acre golf course, game conservancy, beaches, private airstrip, lakes, woodland areas, and nature trails, along with extensive luxury residences. [33] Part of this development was to also "putting in infrastructure such as roads, power and water."

---

[33] Group of risk-taking friends transform plantation into golf haven for Kenya's rich BY DINFIN MULUPI ,10 OCTOBER 2014, How We Made It In Africa online.

- MasterCard Global Destination Cities Index, released in July 2014, listed Africa's top five most traveled to cities which included Johannesburg and Cape Town (South Africa), Cairo (Egypt), Lagos (Nigeria), and Casablanca (Morocco). Not all of the travelers to these cities come from outside the continent. "A large portion of international visitors to Johannesburg come from with southern Africa, with the top five neighbouring feeder countries being Zimbabwe, Lesotho, Mozambique, Botswana and Swaziland respectively." [34]

- For both business and casual travel, mid-priced accommodations are a critical area of expansion as well as a relatively easy market to enter because of the low cost of building in Africa combined with a low-cost, high-quality labor force. Pricewaterhouse Coopers reported on the steady increase in accommodations among several African countries. They reported in part:

> In the South African market, overall spending on rooms in all categories rose 14% in 2013 to R17.3 billion, reflecting an increase in stay unit nights and an 8.4% rise in the average room rate. This publication also features information about hotel accommodation in Nigeria, Mauritius and, for the first time this year, Kenya.

> The hotel market in Nigeria grew 9% in 2013 and by a cumulative 59% over the past four years. Growth has been fuelled by a large increase in available rooms and a rapidly growing economy. Hotel room revenue in Mauritius decreased by 8.7% in 2013 and is projected to grow at 4.6% compounded annually to 2018. Kenya's hotel market

---

[34] Africa's top five most travelled to cities BY KATE DOUGLAS, JULY 2014, How We Made It In Africa online.

declined during the past two years, falling 6.6% in 2012 and by a further 2.6% in 2013. We are very excited to include a detailed analysis of the cruise industry in South Africa for the first time in this year's publication. [35]

- The decline in Kenya's hotel market was mainly due to fears sparked by highly publicized terror attacks from the Somali-based Al-Shabaab group in recent years. The citizens of Nairobi did not project such fears during our summer 2014 visit with the Africa Trade and Link Expo group.

- As was witnessed firsthand during my recent trip to the East African nation of Kenya, urban construction, especially commercial office space, appeared to be booming. To service this rapid expansion of trade and commerce, accommodations businesses are also expanding, thereby creating additional demand for service and industry. *How We Made It In Africa*, one of our favorite online news sources for continental business expansion, shared critical insights into the multiplicity of services that accompany such growth in an article which appeared June 2014, from which the following informative excerpts are shared:

Bobby Sound is a director at TechPro Systems, an interior contractor that has done work for a number of new hotels, lodges and restaurants.

The company started out in 1990 as a hobby for Sound and his father. The duo initially focused on making

---

[35] South African Hospitality Outlook: 2014-2018, Pricewaterhouse Coopers / www.pwc.co.za

handcrafted furniture, but later diversified into doing interior fit-out and metal fabrication.

"Hotels and restaurants are our biggest market because individuals can only afford six chairs or one bed, yet hotels can afford bigger volumes. For instance we supplied 16 tons of furniture to a bush camp in the Maasai Mara when they opened. Selling in larger volumes enables us to offer products at more affordable rates. We are seeing more demand for our services as more new hotels near completion," says Sound.

"The opening of new restaurants are also boosting our business. For instance, we worked with KFC in their three outlets in Nairobi. Lots of franchises are coming to Kenya, like South African brands Adega Restaurants and Ocean Basket. Naturally that is good for us because they require the services of local contractors," he adds. [36]

In concluding this section of my report on the myriad of opportunities for wealth building in African tourism. Specific areas where this inquiry could be much further developed include ecotourism, coastal recreation facilities, health tourism, transport vehicles, mid-priced hotels, educational tours, safari, food service industries, airline support, cruise ships and their related services, cultural and historical experiences, entertainment and much more.

Light and Medium Industrial Manufacturing

As has been so aptly proven about China's phenomenal rapid rise to economic power, low-cost industrial manufacturing is an

---

[36] Kenya's new hotels and restaurants creating opportunities for interior contractors BY DINFIN MULUPI, 25 JUNE 2014 / www.howwemadeitinafrica.com

essential priority for emerging market countries. It has often been claimed that one of the most significant challenges facing Sub-Saharan African nations is reversing the massive export of raw materials in exchange for manufactured goods from those recipient countries who profit tremendously from the trade. Where resource extraction leads to a significant increase in industrial manufacturing using indigenous resources, the building of wealth naturally follows for such nations. This formula is presently serving to bring a considerable transformation to many African national economies.

If one were to look specifically at the *industrial growth rate* happening across the globe, there is reason to get excited about African nations. While we understand that the starting point for these high growth rates is quite low compared to highly industrialized countries, nonetheless, a dawning opportunity is the point of our focus, especially in light of the high rate of growth of consumer populations across Sub-Saharan Africa. According to the *CIA World Factbook 2014*, 16 of the 35 highest industrial production growth rates in the world today are occurring among African nations, with Sierra Leone (*pre*-Ebola crisis), DR Congo, Sudan, Ghana and Chad leading the pack. [37]

What must be noted is that much of this industrial growth is due to the *extraction* industries such as mining, forestry products, oil, and gas production. If these nations are to keep their wealth for their citizens, then industrial manufacturing needs to expand immensely. There is a great reason to be optimistic about such expansion over the coming decades.

---

[37] Country Comparison: Industrial Production Growth Rate, the World Factbook, www.CIA.gov

A spectrum of industrial manufacturing companies is currently emerging from across the continent. The stories associated with these new industrial pioneers are quite impressive.

Over 25 years, beginning at age 18, Kenya-based Heril Bangara developed his manufacturing capacity from manufacturing a modest four plastic water tanks per month to a current industrial empire that produced $24.5 million last year. His company, the Flame Tree Group (FTG), produces water tanks, chemicals, cosmetics, and snacks and has plants in Kenya, Etiopia, Sudan, Rwanda, and Mozambique, along with offices in Burundi employing about 1000 persons across their operations. [38]

As was covered elsewhere in this report, motor vehicle manufacturing in Africa is growing at an impressive rate. A spectrum of motor vehicles, including autos, trucks, SUVs, motorcycles, urban transport buses and luxury buses are being built in Nigeria, Ghana, Tanzania, Uganda, South Africa, Morocco, and Kenya. The African Automotive Design Association is a group that includes "Automotive designers, Artists, Architects, craft persons, students, and enthusiasts, who seek to promote Africa's rich culture and heritage through the study of automotive design." An examination of their website (which can be accessed at www.AfricanAutoMotiveDesign.blogspot.com) can certainly lead one to a great excitement about the unlimited potential of African domestic motor vehicle production. [39]

Concerning agricultural production across Africa, one of the challenges to be overcome to reach full potential is the problem of food spoilage. According to the UN's Food and Agriculture Organization, in parts of Sub-Saharan Africa experience rates of

---

[38] An East African manufacturer's journey from modest start-up to listed company BY DINFIN MULUPI ,4 NOVEMBER 2014 / How We Made It In Africa
[39] Who or What is AADA?, from The African Automotive Design Association, Jan. 2007 / http://africanautomotivedesign.blogspot.com

food spoilage as high as 50%, resulting in loss of "enough food annually to feed 300 million, or nearly a third of all of Sub-Saharan Africa." [40] One of the solutions to this problem is to create food processing and storage facilities much closer to the rural areas that are the heart of nations' agricultural production.

Through the online micro-lending organization Kiva.org we have the case of a Ugandan woman, Grace Ayaa, who received a small loan of $400 with which she purchased a grinding machine to process locally grown peanuts into peanut butter, as well as a refrigerator for storage. Her small business was so successful that she was able to extract a respectable income. Her inspiring story was highlighted in a PBS.org Frontline World documentary. [41] This is a case where light manufacturing can make a massive difference in the outcome for an entire neighborhood for a minimal sum of money.

Grace Ayaa's example can be duplicated an innumerable number of times across a vast scale of development. I have myself inquired as to machines produced in China and India that can be imported into Africa for a low cost. These small-scale food processors can produce juice and other fruit products that can ultimately be distributed and exported. The possibilities are not limited to food and agriculture. Auto parts, furniture, apparel, small appliances, nutritional and medicinal herbs, musical instruments, sporting goods, recreational facilities, beverages, computer parts, and many other light-to-medium industrial products will be increasingly manufactured within the nations that now produce raw resources at tremendous rates. This is the future of an industry that promises to unleash a long-suppressed

---

[40] SRI: Food Waste & Spoilage in Sub-Saharan Africa, 2013 /
http://mongabay.org/
[41] Micro Lending is Sweet, by Jaime Acosta, Huffington Post online edition, Mar. 28, 2008

expansion of African economic might that will lead to an anticipated and predicted superpower status for a united African economic order. By the end of the 21st Century, this should likely lead to heavy industry and the highest level of technology.

When countries like China, Korea, India, and Iran can move, within a century, from colonial exploitation and extreme poverty to now competing as industrial and high-tech centers of a newly emerging global economic order, let us not restrict our own imaginations as to the high possibility that African nations will also join this technical and commercial wave of growth and development and that this will occur during our lifetime.

Chapter 11 – Three Pan African Agenda Priorities

We can never honestly engage these investigations and conversations about the future of our global family without coming to concrete solutions based upon an accurate reading of the vast amount of information that we have uncovered. While there is a strong tendency on the part of too many of our "culturally conscious community" to engage in constant pessimism and fear-mongering, many of us do not allow such negativity to serve as our standard. I am convinced and will argue the case any time the challenge arises, that there is an undeniable basis for such optimism that will lead to deliberate and immediate actions. I will take a brief portion of this document to share just why I have become so excited about these developments.

Here are three primary agenda priorities that will significantly jumpstart momentum toward achieving fundamental goals of our futurist forecasts for the milestone years of 2030 (an extensive and impactful African agricultural expansion) and 2050 (arrival at an African population of 2 billion mostly middle-class population, continental federation and subsequently, the achieving of superpower status).

Restoration of the Value of Black Labor

From the dawn of human civilization, it was the *value of black labor* that is credited with creating culture, dynamic economic structures, and agriculture-based societies. Black labor was crucial at the development of high civilizations, such as that which dominated the world from the Nile River Valley for more than

10,000 years. Purdue University professor Jules Janick stated as fact: "Ancient Egypt is shown to be the source of much of the agricultural technology of the Western World." [42]

It was a combination of indigenous African agricultural knowledge along with the transportation of 10's of millions of African laborers during the trans-Atlantic slave trade that developed the Western Hemisphere into the mercantile basis of global economic dominance. It was black labor that produced the most valuable crops on the planet at that time: sugar, tobacco, and cotton. Experienced rice farmers from West Africa brought their knowledge to the U.S. and built one of the world's most significant rice production and exportation systems. Here's what one historical source cited in Wikipedia has to say on the early history of rice production in the U.S.:

> The colonial South Carolina and Georgia prospered and amassed great wealth from the slave labor obtained from the Senegambia area of West Africa and from coastal Sierra Leone. One batch of slaves was advertised as "a choice cargo of Windward and Gold Coast Negroes, who have been accustomed to the planting of rice." At the port of Charleston, through which 40% of all American slave imports passed, slaves from Africa brought the highest prices in recognition of their prior knowledge of rice culture, which was put to use on the many rice plantations around Georgetown, Charleston, and Savannah. [43]

It was black labor that built the U.S. system to become the most significant agricultural export economy that dominated the 20th Century. It was the migration of black labor away from the

---

[42] Ancient Egyptian Agriculture and the Origins of Horticulture, by Jules Janick, Dept. of Horticulture and Landscape Architecture, Purdue University
[43] Rice and Slavery: A Fatal Gold Seede, by Jean M. West // citation from Wikipedia

terrorist-filled geography of the southern agrarian belt into the industrial cities of the north and west, which provided the labor reserve to fuel the national industrial expansion. This black labor reserve stepped into the factories (along with a female labor reserve) during World War II. It allowed America's industrial production to rise to world dominance so that the nation emerged from the conflict which destroyed its European and Asian competitors as the undeniable champion of the industrial output.

Black labor shows up at every phase of America's rise to then-unchallenged economic dominance. Yet, when American corporations, through their greedy short-sightedness, began to undermine the urban centers (which were becoming increasingly dominated by urban demographics which allowed for black political domination) by exporting the industries which thrived on inexpensive but high-quality labor, the fate of the nation slowly turned around. Today we see the consequence of 4 decades of outsourcing of American manufacturing primarily to regions of the planet which supply low-cost, high-value labor. While these powerful corporations have pulled this trick on the nation, to the detriment of the middle-class labor force, we should be able to determine that the ultimate outcome of this will never serve our economic interests and thus come up with countermeasures which can reverse this fate that is devastating our economic development.

I contend that we still possess within our hands the ability to determine vast economic development. I have done all that I can over recent months to communicate this understanding to all that will listen, that our people, especially the urban youth, have the potential to create an exciting new economic dynamic based upon our realization of the remarkable historical power of *black labor*. The best way to demonstrate this power and our understanding of it is to set into place a myriad of systems that combine this wealth-producing black labor with available resources.

A Return to Agriculture-Based Societies

For some six years now, I have collaborated with a series of black-owned farmland communities under what we call the *Kujichagulia Village Development Projects*. In a significant report that I published one year ago: ***KUJICHAGULIA VILLAGES: A Practical Plan for Self-Determination***, we explored in great detail a strategic initiative to create a series of *intentional communities* and to develop within these sites a spectrum of some 110 identified economic activities that would restore productivity, self-sufficiency and sovereign development to participants. [44]

Kujichagulia Villages are a practical plan for self-Reparations to evolve.

The key to the success of the Kujichagulia Village Projects is a broad-based return to rural community development. For far too many Afri-Amers, urban living had become too expensive, dangerous, and chaotic for us to sustain over the coming decades. The vast amount of underutilized black labor within the urban ghetto communities that could be converted into so many different industrial activities was shocking to many people who read that report. Yet, what was being pointed out in the document was that our people already had vast experience in developing such resources. The report dealt with housing, education, cultural tourism, handicrafts, agricultural production, healing facilities, systems for self-governance, land acquisition as

---

[44] KUJICHAGULIA VILLAGES: A Practical Plan for Self-Determination, by Keidi Awadu / The Conscious Rasta Report Vol. 7 No. 2, July 2013

well as marketing our extensive set of products and services to our urban-connected communities and the world.

For so many reasons, this restoration of rural agriculture-based societies seems so practical and reasonable. Yet, there is tremendous resistance from urban dwellers to such a radical transition from the areas where they have become accustomed to living. This resistance persists despite the widespread condemnation on the part of many urban dwellers of the lifestyle patterns which they observe all around them in daily life. One of my primary motivations for persisting with the advocacy of such a program of reverse-migration is solely due to the gross underutilization of the urban black labor force. Not only do we witness vast man-hours of wasted labor value, but many of the urban lifestyle patterns work conversely to our stated aims of using our economic potential for sustainable development.

Many urban dwellers consumption patterns of bad food, toxicity due to illicit drugs and alcohol, debt-financing for housing and transportation, over-consumption of degenerate media, pointless consumerism, as well as being caught up in a vast and debilitating criminal justice system – all of these and more combine to deliver us as a mostly unsustainable community. The collapse of these urban centers, which have the highest concentration of black populations, stands as stark evidence that a significant change must occur to stave off future (and permanent) catastrophic collapse. We see evidence of this collapse in once black-governed cities like Detroit, Philadelphia, Baltimore, Washington DC, New York City, Kansas City, Cleveland, Pittsburg, Atlanta, and many others; not all of these cities are in general collapse, but one could argue that the black communities reflect a grand failure.

As I stated in **KUJICHAGULIA VILLAGES**, Blacks in America sacrificed as much as 85% of their farmlands during the 20th Century, mainly due to urban migration and other economic factors. Recovery of this farmland has been little or no priority in the vast majority of conversations that take place on what to do about the urban economic plight and the dilemma faced by black youth and adult workers. Without a plan to correct this historical failure, there is very little reasonable chance that a turnaround in our economic, political, and social fate can take place. Just the amount of depletion of our sovereign economic potential which is being drained by our disproportionate engagement in a vast prison-industrial complex likely amounts to "between $ 20 and $35 billion annually, and one report has more than 523,000 full-time employees working in American corrections-more than in any Fortune 500 company except General Motors." [45]

Because this prison population is disproportionately made up of black laborers, this is resulting in an *economic reversal* of what I estimate to be over $60 billion annually IF those prisoners could be converted to fully productive participants in the nation's labor market at average productivity.

One of the primary means of correcting the set of behaviors that have served up so many of our youth for the incarceration industries would be to remove them from the corrupted and stressful environments where such maladaptive actions are widespread. By creating vibrant, hopeful, productive and educational communities like the Kujichagulia Villages, the youth can have a renewed sense of self-esteem, respect for their valued status within a supportive community, hands-on training in valuable vocations as well as a place within which their natural creative talents can be fully expressed. Those of us who have spent time in the countryside, have had a chance to bring forth Life from sun-drenched soils, create sovereign systems for

---

[45] Big Bucks from the Big House: The prison industrial complex and beyond, excerpted from the book Lockdown America: Police and Prisons in the Age of Crisis, by Christian Parenti, Verso Books, 1999

community development, and celebrated de-stressing from urban life, we do know the enormous potential of such a movement on a grand scale. This could be one of the most significant changes in the broader community since the rural-to-urban migration that occurred a century earlier.

Transforming Consumers to Producers

Another critical area that must become a central focus for reversing this vast degeneration we are witnessing is the need to break the cycle of *consumerism* that has plagued our people since the mid-1960s and the achievement of "civil rights" and political inclusion. This plague of consumerism has become so common and widespread that many don't even recognize the trend as it manifests in our daily activities or what the long-term consequences of such continued behaviors present to the individual and the group.

The range of products which are consumed which do not result in long term empowerment is too much for this section of this report to fully articulate. This has been well documented in many different sources, including this and other publications I have created over the years. What is most alarming is the way that we have been *trained to think* in moving naturally toward consumption without even considering that we should be (or *could be*) producing as much or more than we consume. If the behavior of Afri-Amers as a group, considering the ratio of consumption versus production, were projected upon any corporation competing in the marketplace, then that corporation would be undeniably headed toward bankruptcy (except for the United States of America, Inc. which can print money out of nothing and use such funds to perpetuate itself).

I recently had a conversation with a group of people regarding the new state of IPTV (Internet-Protocol Television) developments and the immediate future ahead. As I was excitedly telling the group about what YouTube and Google have recently put on the table that will lead to a whole new level of media development, I turned to two teenaged black men who were in the room. I asked them to tell the group what they thought about YouTube. They became excited and animated at the topic and that the adults in the room were genuinely interested in something which holds their fascination. It was easy for these youth to express the importance of YouTube videos in their world and among their peers. They also seemed to hint that few adults appreciated the significance of the amount of pride that youth took in seeing their peers in such a free-expression environment.

When I redirected the conversation slightly from *consuming* YouTube videos to another section of the enterprise called "YouTube Space," their eyes drew a blank in response. YT Space represents the frontier of the *producer* side of the media giant. Unfortunately for these youth and every adult in the room other than myself, we have focused too much on the consumption value of such online media outlets and not given much attention at all on how to become the producers. The same is true with an annual investment of $80 billion in consumption from "full-service supermarkets" by Afri-Amers. Such a substantial yearly contribution to this sector could very well be the basis of numerous group-owned supermarket corporations and employment of a vast network of employees along with vertically-integrated support businesses.

Personal care products, home finance, and other lending products, alcohol consumption, recreation activities (including sports and travel), fashion and apparel, autos and transportation, cable, satellite and IPTV media subscriptions, healthcare services, seasonal shopping, utilities, restaurants, higher education and much more – these sectors all have the potential to be redirected from mere consumption to include vast production as well. How Afri-Amers have tolerated an entrenched leadership class that has not successfully acted upon this imperative is almost beyond comprehension. What is increasingly being understood is that these patterns of behavior are unsustainable and within a few generations have come to put the entire ethnic class in great danger of obsolescence and increased omission and exclusion from the national economic outlook.

We have got to face the fact that, despite a vast network of HBCU's (Historically Black Colleges and Universities), advanced degrees, leadership organizations, religious societies, fraternal organizations, journalists, media outlets, and other structures that reach and direct our people, we have dismally *failed* to secure our vast resources and assure that such assets are applied to both group and individual priorities and long-term behavioral patterns in an ultimately sustainable manner.

Many of you will read and completely agree with everything that is being written herein. Your comprehension is the affirmation that we can indeed do much better. What remains is the strength of the structure that we have planned and put into place that will directly and appropriately address the challenges that have been stated. My, your, or anyone else's complaining about these subjects has already proven to be an inadequate response to an enormous deficit between our patterns of consumption versus production. From this point onward, we *demand and expect* appropriate planning and concentration of the resources (along with skilled black labor) to repair our past mistakes and to forge another pathway to the future. "By any means necessary," we command our collective to a new set of plans, behaviors, investments, and outcomes. The legacy that we would leave future generations demands that we act immediately.

Chapter 12 – AFRICA RISING – We Got Next

A broad spectrum of research on the general topic of **"Africa Rising"** has increasingly been appearing throughout the press over the past two decades now. These pieces are not merely wishful thinking on the part of self-declared "Pan Africans." Much of this rise in such optimistic African economics forecasts we are witnessing is published within some of the top scholarly institutions in the world. The spectrum of indicators that feed this theme of optimism includes numerous sectors that we have discussed throughout this report: energy, mining, agriculture, healthcare, development capital infusion, technology expansion, demographics, industrial growth, travel and tourism, improved governance, conflict resolution and improved wealth stratification within societies.

As well, within each of particular sectors, there are numerous stories of how companies and individuals are carving out their niche and making tremendous fortunes from their ability to develop trans-national economic investments into long term gain. I have become convinced that several nations are wonderfully positioned to be able to make this next leap from the deficits left behind because of the long experiences of the trans-Atlantic enslavement, a century of colonial plunder, being subject to the worst of the Cold War hostilities, and the impact of post-Cold War economic policies of resource extraction, debt burden, poor governance, and covert subterfuge.

I am particularly impressed with gains within certain nations such as Ghana, Nigeria, Senegal, Kenya, South Africa, Angola, Botswana, Zambia, Zimbabwe, Uganda, Rwanda, Ethiopia, Central African Republic, Tanzania and others that are more recently emerging from the crises imposed by the negative impact of those experiences earlier noted. Perched on the edge of rapid and sustainable rise as well are nations such as the Gambia, the Dem. Republic of the Congo, Eritrea, Cameroon, and perhaps even Sudan. While this report almost completely ignores the North Africa region called the Maghreb, which is dominated by Arab and Mediterranean allegiances, there is no doubt that the northern region also has some promising lights.

Beyond the current and anticipated successes by individuals, companies, trans-national corporations, and individual nations, I am convinced that the most significant opportunity for African progress lies in the regional blocks. The Africa Union has designated five large *Regional Economic Communities (REC's)* for the continent of 55 nations consisting of the Arab-dominated north (1) the Arab Maghreb Union – UMA, (2) Economic Community of West African States – ECOWAS, (3) Economic Community of Central African States – ECCAS, (4) Southern African Development Community – SADC, and (5) East African Community – EAC.

Additionally, there is also input from outside the African continent in support of African Union policies from a sixth region encompassing the African Diaspora. However, it must be noted that this sixth region consists of competing groups, is not united, and has too little influence on continental African affairs. This is not to say that the Diaspora African groups might not form a functional unity shortly and provide a substantial contribution to the sustainable development that we are currently witnessing.

Within each of these RECs, there are wonderfully bright lights rising. Each of the regions has one or more core states which are doing quite well. As these nations increase their integration, cooperation, and sharing of industrial development, we are surely going to witness the rise of new *"superstates."* There is indeed a great reason to be optimistic about these developments concerning the RECs. I am convinced that it will be within the Regional Economic Communities and their continued interrelated development that we will see this great continental superpower state come into practical existence. For the next 25 years or so we should be looking for ways to bolster regional development, capital investment expansion, growth of Small and Medium-sized Enterprises (SME's), development of light-to-heavy industries, agricultural and agribusiness expansion, transportation and communication capacity, increased electrification, energy development, security cooperation, cultural exchange as well as increased access and standardization of higher education.

The brilliant Senegalese scientist Dr. Cheikh Anta Diop forecast these developments and laid out an excellent set of strategies in his book, ***BLACK AFRICA: The Economic and Cultural Basis for a Federated State***. This book is highly recommended for those who want to comprehend more about the needed substructures for the practical implementation of the integrated continental state, which is the goal of most Pan African advocates. The book was published in 1974 and imagined a 25-year strategic plan that would deliver the powerful Federated African Republic to the world. It was an incredibly brilliant plan which the overwhelming majority of African leadership, as well as most self-styled Pan Africans, wholly overlooked.

Highlights of Dr. Diop's strategic plan included the following basics:

- Restoration and development of a historical consciousness that would also include linguistic unity, political realignment and return to traditional governing structures;

- Extensive electrification and energy expansion across the continent, to include a spectrum of energy sources with great emphasis on renewable energy sources;

- Each of the various economic communities developing industries based upon unique natural resources and transportation potential;

- Development capital investment funding, scientific research, as well as "14 Steps to African Unity".

Around the world, other nations are contributing to African development in ways quite distinct from the experiences of enslavement, colonial, neo-colonial, and hostile intervention. For decades Cuba has been a bold and decisive agent helping nations to emerge from the dominance of hostile external powers and vulture capitalism. It was the partnership of Cuba along with Angola, Namibia, and South African freedom fighters that stood down the powerful Apartheid domination of the SA Defense Forces, which had previously imposed their will on the entire southern portion of the continent.

Brazil is increasingly a development partner with the former Portuguese colonies with which they have linguistic and cultural ties, such as Angola, Mozambique, Guinea-Bissau, Equatorial Guinea, and Cape Verde. As the economic status of Portugal continues to stagnate, increasingly Brazil seems to be stepping into a strong position of influence over the former colonies. As part of the powerful BRICS block of nations which appears to comprise the emerging economic bloc to challenge and supersede the waning European powers, there is no denying that Brazil, along with China and Russia, is a significant competitor to the western powers. As well, in the western hemisphere, Brazil is the undisputed economic rival to the U.S., which is increasingly being pushed out of partnerships with numerous nations, mainly due to the nasty history of Cold War manipulation that was instigated at the hands of U.S. security policies.

Across the African continent, one can see plays for power, position, trade, and influence from emerging Asian nations. China is the most obvious example of such presence, but others, such as India, Russia, South Korea, and Indonesia, cannot be overlooked as well as Israel. Quite simply, Africa has an abundance of natural resources and energy-producing potential, of which every expanding economy in the world wants to partake.

From throughout the non-continental Diaspora, there is reason to be optimistic that black individuals, groups, organizations, companies, and universities are also coming into full awareness of this rapidly developing African potential. I have traveled to the continent on six occasions with three separate groups that have become energized over the future potential of the continent and our critical role in seeing this destiny come to full fruition. Members of these trips have been encouraged to contribute to continental associations, education, real estate development, technology, capital investment, business partnerships, mechanical engineering, and industrial development. We have donated many times with material supplies as well as transferred technology to the continent. Plans are to seriously upgrade our capacity for technology transfer as well as a supply of technical know-how to develop and manage the systems required to run modern nations.

As the many predictions shared within this report indicate, there will continue to rise the need for a spectrum of new partners, skilled technicians, expanded education, and human resource development. The vast set of experiences that Diaspora Africans have acquired through our centuries of the journey since the time of the Maafa has endowed us with the potential to assist greatly toward the organization of the great African superpower state the likely will emerge by 2050. We have a lot of tough work ahead of us, but history has shown that we are indeed a people capable of such impressive transformation.

Chapter 13 – Do African Americans Have a Viable Future?

There have been so many frightening predictions for Blacks in the United States and other Diaspora countries. While temporal concerns may range from urban violence to infectious diseases, some areas have been mainly overlooked wherein there is a great reason to be concerned.

I do my best to stay out of the camp that is often accused of the "Chicken Little syndrome." Some people are afraid of *everything or something* at any given time. Much of this misdirected fear and anxiety is a consequence of consuming too much television news, which seems to be obsessed with promoting anything that will cause paranoia among its audience. As well, conspiracies run amok on the Internet, late-night radio, and make for popular subject matter among lecture circuits and private conversations.

While there is a great reason to be cautious about many of the topics that commonly cross our minds, it seems to this researcher that too often we're obsessed with trivial matters, such as minute details about celebrity lifestyles, or with impractical subjects with which we can likely do little or nothing actually to improve our lives.

All that said, I want to plant a few seeds of caution within your mind that could likely have a powerful impact on your and my fate over the decades ahead. Let's begin with the possibility of adverse events that are likely to impact the lives of many of those for whom this book is being written.

1. **Our group's demographic trends are working against us.** There are numerous indicators that the black family in the U.S., Europe, the Caribbean, and Canada is floundering. We

have seen a steep decline in marriage rates over recent decades, and it seems unlikely that this trend will reverse itself; to the contrary, it is still getting worse. The number of childbirths per female has dropped well below replacement rate and held at that point for decades, again unlikely to reverse toward positive trend (in direct contradiction to our African continental cousins' favorable demographics).

When birthrates drop so low for so long, the group then experiences "population aging," which is generally considered a burden on the society as there are not enough young people producing enough surplus for the elderly to be adequately taken care of. Abortion rates among all American women are disproportionately impacting our group and Afri-Amers have cumulatively misplaced a third of their population due to this one cause since the legalization and popularization of the unholy practice in 1973; a historic decline in population that is equivalent to the disappearance of 600 million continental Africans due to the trans-Atlantic slave trade. The net sum of these trends portends the demise of as many as 92% of our childbirths by the year 2065.

2. **The gross disproportion of our young workers who have become killed, incarcerated, or otherwise removed from the labor force.** Societies thrive from the fruits of labor, and the most valuable contribution to society is that provided by the younger workforce. Least we would overlook the historical parallel, during the time of the slave trade in the Americas, it was the young black male and childbearing age female who were regarded as the most valuable chattel property; this because they were expected to produce many years of high-value / low-cost labor throughout their lives. Today, that value has been reversed, and these same youth are portrayed

as a burden upon society as well as within many families.

Rather than producing an average of nearly $70,000 annually in the labor market, an incarcerated citizen is warehoused at about half that amount for years, even decades at a time. Younger and older inmates are also more expensive. Thus we have a reversal from productive labor to a non-productive drain on society and community. While a restored valuation to black work could be orchestrated in a relatively short time, there seems to be at present a general lack of innovative and creative imagination or commitment to composing such a plan that would succeed at reversing this trend.

3. **Our community members consume far more than they produce.** There is no escaping the fact that America is a nation obsessed with *consumerism*. Yet, when we regard the various ethnic groups for patterns of consumption, income savings, wealth accumulation, debt participation, and business expansion, we appear to be at or near the negative end of all of these trends. Wise and prudent people save their money, stay away from usury and debt, purchase in manners which maximize return on investment, provide for their children's economic welfare, secure their own basic needs, and own the real estate within which their communities are built. I think it seems pretty evident that this description *does not* fit the general impression of our ethnic group in America. It is shameful to bear witness to the widespread patterns of consumer behavior attributed to the black community.

4. **In general, Afri-Amers are out of sync with historical times.** Too often, our youth, and the adults as well, have little workable familiarity with history. While the psychic trauma of

enslavement, Jim Crow, racial exclusion, urban uprisings, media-propagandized inferiority, failing civic education and criminal injustices have all served to justify a desire for historical and cultural amnesia, there is no record of any group surviving through good times or bad without having a strong foundation of self-identity and pride which goes with maintaining their distinct history. Because of this lack of historical awareness, the ability to see "over the horizon" and to predict what are long term outcomes of short term policies is severely inhibited. When a group is out of sync with historical time, it likely appears that they may be nearing the demise of their foundation for staying committed to the group. It has become quite apparent to some of us that the Afri-Amer community, led by widespread media distortion of affairs impacting or *seeming* to affect the group, doesn't maintain sufficient focus on any particular news topic for more than a few weeks or months before we are fed something else to obsess over. Our memories seem to be a bit more reliable about sports, entertainment, and other less essential affairs.

5. **Information served to us distorts our sense of self-preservation** – The current crisis in urban education, which has produced an entire generation of youth unprepared to be productive members of the broader economic, social and political order has become all too apparent when one examines a variety of trends regarding social development. From the generalized *socialization* which children gain from a pre-school, elementary, secondary and higher education; to the ways that our community members have seemingly *un-learned* how to incorporate science and mathematics practically in their lives; to the manner of programming which has too many of our higher education graduates merely

seeking to compete for jobs in a workforce environment where most don't even work within their specific field of education of which they majored. It might appear that either these various fields of knowledge are failing to serve our community, or conversely, that our people have had unrealistic expectations when it comes to getting the most out of the public education system.

Additionally, throughout life, continuing education does naturally occur even unto the advanced ages. Yet, sources of this constant infusion of information that would serve Afri-Amers has a significant impact on the ultimate outcome of such information, how it creates societal access, as well as our ability to utilize what we have learned practically. As we witness the generalized trend of moving away from literacy attainment toward consumption of higher amounts of electronic entertainment, sports, and gaming, we also see the degradation of our capacity as critical thinkers, sovereign producers, and reliable community partners. Obviously, there is a direct correlation between the amount of television consumption and the quality of productive citizen that is created within any community.

While I could go on with many of these negative trends which are impacting current lives and the future prospects for Afri-Amers (and I have already begun another book which lists 15 specific trends that *must* be reversed for the group to recover its long term viability), I want to avoid getting trapped into what I commonly refer to as the *scarcity principle*, which is seeing everything as unfavorable and excluding the energizing impact of witnessing a contrary *abundance principle*. I am at heart an optimist, and this energy is best sustained by seeing the positive potential as generally more of a natural order of human evolvement. Therefore, let me put some ideas into the mind of you, the reader, that demonstrate why this group I am referring to as *Afri-Amers*has grounds to be optimistic about a viable future despite continuous waves of bad news all around.

1. **A unique and challenging history has shaped Afri-Amers –** Contrary to the foundation of slavery and oppression as a basis for identity, I like to think of our history at this point as one who has refined a potential personality to which we could draw the analogy of how steel is made: it takes a lot of heat and addition of rare elements to turn iron into the most durable steel.

    It is often suggested that we have the potential to make the best Pan African advocates because we carry bloodlines from all of the indigenous continental populations (so-called *tribes*), and thus can imagine unity and unified action across nations and locations. I will add to this that our having survived so many of the horrors and deprivations put upon us through these centuries of oppression has made us resilient, creative, resourceful, skilled in multiple fields, and sensitive to the possibility of danger if we would make mistakes along our pathway.

    One can see in the wisdom preserved by the elders among us as evidence of much of this practical resilience. I love to listen to stories of how previous generations faced so many hostile challenges but still managed to maintain their productivity, sense of the value of self, and moral integrity. From these lessons, I get inspired to want to create and pass on a similar legacy for my posterity. Quite honestly, I see Afri-Amers as talented survivors, resistant to trivial obsessions, and focused on the health of our families in a way that most people could not possibly understand. Are these sentiments common within our ethnicity currently? Probably *not*. Yet, I remain convinced that this awareness is not buried too deeply within the collective psyche of our people and could be revived with the right type of public awareness campaign.

2. **We have among our members skilled and experienced knowledge in all functions of a modern complex society** – If given the task of taking inventory of all of the fields for which Afri-Amers have extensive working knowledge and critical leadership experience, this list would be quite comprehensive. It would undoubtedly include human relations, politics, governance, healthcare, transportation infrastructure, automobile design and manufacturing, agriculture, food processing, market distribution, fashion industries, entertainment, media production, education, invention, advanced scientific research, geometrics (measuring Earth and the natural elements), energy production, city planning, military affairs, spirituality, child-rearing, computer technology, and information management systems.

In other words, members of our "Noble Race" have experience in *every* aspect of managing advanced industrial and information-based societies. Should we be able to either confirm this vast amount of expert first-hand knowledge into a well-organized structure to serve our ethnic group here in the U.S., *or* to transfer this body of industrial wisdom to friendly and supportive governments across the African world, we would undeniably be one of the most considerable resources to become available to such nations in the last half-millennium. Through our Kujichagulia Villages projects, we have been developing bases for developing and coordinating such talent here on domestic soils with the long term vision of being able to use these sites as academies to train world leadership based in no small measure on this broad set of working knowledge that we have accumulated.

3. **As U.S. citizens, we have access to immense resources** – While there seems to be a predominating mindset that we are held back in America, the truth is that our group of 45 million Afri-Amers is the wealthiest and best-educated mass of Africans on the planet. We have access to excellent capital flow (despite that we have been *trained* to be consumers and not competitive producers) that serves as the actual profitability of some of the wealthiest corporations on this planet.

When Afri-Amers contribute $40 to $50 billion annually in increased spending during the holiday shopping season [updated to $67.2 billion during Nov-Dec 2020], it is within this margin that many corporations thrive, survive or go out of business that year. This very same sum is the literal equivalent of what China spent across the whole African continent in 2013 for which they received a 5-to-1 return on their investment in trade and commerce with Africa. Our annual contribution to full-service supermarkets in the U.S. amounts to $80 billion annually, indeed a sufficient amount for us to purchase or build a highly competitive supermarket chain in the country.

All U.S. citizens can go into the federal patent office and pull from a spectrum of publicly available plans and blueprints to develop high technology and industrial products. I have an excellent life history of spending hundreds if not thousands of hours within some of the superb college libraries in the country, including UCLA, USC, Emory University, and Johns

Hopkins. Even the local libraries have vast stores of books, magazines, and online resources that could be used as a basis for a robust, self-developing education.

While there is a great reason to consider that our military experience as citizens of this country has left us lacking for group development, nonetheless such experience would be valuable if it were made available for developing countries that need to have their domestic security bolstered by such workable knowledge and expertise. Similarly, with scientific circles, we can gain first-hand access to learning in a spectrum of advanced fields of research and future development. Given the task, I am sure that I could list 100 advantages that Afri-Amers could draw upon because we are legal citizens of the country that is currently the wealthiest and most technologically advanced society in the world.

4. **We are a people highly loved and appreciated around the world** – Despite the common belief among many of our members that we are despised, excluded and treated as unwanted interlopers, there is a great reason to reverse that perspective. I have traveled extensively across the U.S. in addition to 15 other countries. I have undeniably been insulted and excluded based upon my African ethnic inheritance. Yet, when compared to the broad-based experience of such vast travel, I can claim that I am positively received *at least* ten times more than I am rejected. Personal habits undoubtedly have much impact on this positive reception. Still, I contend that, with proper social and psychological training, we are loved and received by everyone who appreciates our unique talents, ability to be resilient and adaptive, and our general kindness toward strangers (the opposite of the *xenophobic* fear of "others" that seems to

permeate the American psyche).

In fields of human creative endeavor, we excel and have long been welcomed as creatively talented in the highest order. When I've traveled outside of America, my experiences have been more than 90 percent welcoming and receptive; it helps that when I am abroad, I try my best to understand the local culture and customs as well as make some effort to speak the local language.

One thing that is very apparent when examining other societies is that they have high regard for distinctly Afri-Amer cultural patterns involving music, fashion, dance, cuisine, artwork, celebrity, outstanding athletic performance, and a general sense of "hipness." This appreciation of the cultural trends which are developed by the Afri-Amer ethnic class becomes even more apparent when you observe the behaviors of young people within African urban societies. We are far more influential than we might imagine, especially if we have never experienced the benefits of international travel.

5. **We are poised to be part of the most significant change in civilization evolution in 2000 years** – Despite constant protest to the contrary, let me shout this out to all who might understand: WE ARE AFRICAN PEOPLE! As such, we are far, far from an impoverished *minority*, and we need to change the language we use to reflect our membership in the world's fastest-growing population, which also harbors the fastest-growing middle class along with industrialization. Who among us would deny the value of Asians seeing themselves as Chinese, Japanese, or Indian first, especially when there is widespread acceptance of their ethnicity and the optimal

position that these groups' members have created for themselves within any nation that they inhabit?

Well, the fact is that in the year 2050, long after America has fallen upon its own sword of self-inflicted degeneration, the African continent will harbor almost one of every four people on the planet; will still enjoy vast open spaces with plenty of natural resources, wildlife, and flora; will have been electrified, energized and excited about the myriad of possibilities now available after centuries of injury at the hands of external powers. By that time, Africa will have secured its citizens. It will be celebrating continued sustainable lifestyles that include an abundance of work, play, spectacular traditions, along with the unbound sentiment that results from constant exposure to the sound of children's joyful laughter throughout the land.

As the population of Black Africa is forecast to *double* by 2050 to 2 billion, it would be no problem at all for such an expansion of 1 billion to include the wealthiest and best-educated Africans from across the planet which might number as many as 50 to 100 million that would be emigrating from Diaspora locations. When compared to the gross deprivation and exclusion, violent oppression and rapid aging of populations within the U.S., U.K., Europe, Canada and other nations where our prospects are marginal, it might seem that the decision to migrate into a future predicted to produce a *superpower* state might present us with an incredible opportunity to enjoy sustainable security and prosperity.

Allow me to answer my question: "Do Afri-Amers have a place in the 22nd Century? Undeniably, YES! Part of moving into this empowered future is also to reset the world calendar forward to its most ancient measurement of human civilization progress. It is right now the 63rd Century KMT (Khemet Time). The world's oldest solar calendar was developed and utilized for over 4200 years BCE (before the *contemporary* Christian era).

So we do have the potential to consolidate our best position for the 22nd Century and then create a new globally accepted concept that we have re-established ourselves projected 42 centuries into the future, which is in reality NOW!

I could write another book on what such a historical realignment with the ancient civilization might entail. There are plenty of books which have done a great job of doing so. It was one such book by the noted scholar Anthony Browder, **Nile Valley Contributions to Civilization**[46] , which served as one of the critical entry points in my awakened learning experience. This book opened up a vast comprehension of societal affairs to me. It is one of the most highly recommended books on African civilization that exists today.

Beyond Browder's brilliant tome, there are thousands of publications to further study that give us perspective on the immense potential of indigenous African civilization development. We learn about the development of *numerous* great African civilizations throughout history, including such great empires as Kush, Khemet, Auxum, Zimbabwe, Kongo, Angola, Mali, Songhai, Ashanti, Ghana, Ibo, Zulu, and others. We come to comprehend that the footprints of our journeys around the planet still are to be beheld as our civilizing influence on world history is unmistakable and undeniable. As I pointed out within this book and in a recent presentation called *Paradigm Shift*, our impact as skilled labor has been the very crux by which the U.S. ascended to become a dominant agricultural, economic, and military superpower. This wealth is a status which the U.S. has

---

[46] Biography of Anthony T. Browder / http://aalbc.com

enjoyed for the majority of the last 100 years of civilization history.

We have built great civilization many times before. It is our mission and high intention to return to this process of civilization advancement. Civilization always is comprised of common cultures banded together to form an even greater entity. Thus our primary tasks center around the comprehension and consolidation of ethnic commonality on the regional, sub-national, national, international, and global scale.

Within the U.S., we have such an enormous task to bring forward progressive cultural environments within the cities, then to join these ventures together across the broader geography. Unique opportunities lie within northern versus southern communities, the cities of the east coast versus the Midwestern agricultural belt, desert regions, and the west coast.

Ultimately many of the very same tools which have been used to make us non-competitors (i.e., mass media, public education, consumer patterns, and choices of entertainment) are the very same mechanisms that can serve to unleash this new dynamic of explosive self-development.

In the earlier chapter entitled "**The Solution, Determined by the Problem**," I brought this idea forward, and now I am hoping that you, the reader can see this in a much clearer light. So at this point, we don't need to crowd our heads with too much detail on why our optimism is moving us forward. At this point, I'm just going to relate further instruction in a phrase which has been heard many times within our community:

JUST DO THE DAMN THING!

STEAM SHIPS
Is the ideal education for our children to capture the future!
Science
Technology
Engineering
Arts
Mathematics
Spirituality
Holistic-Health
Innovation
Prosperity
Sustainaility
AFRICA 2020
Within this STEAM-SHIPS acronym for educating our youth to success, most of these components have direct correspondence within the vast expansion of African agricultural economics, which is the central theme of this book. It is well-established that governments across the continent are committed to these education paradigms as they are also committed to considerable expansion of agroeconomic development and sustainability.
www.TheBlackestSoil.com

Appendix 1 – Agriculture Panel Discussion Points

Presented by Keidi Awadu August 2014 at the 4th Annual Pan African Economic Summit, Los Angeles, California

1. Recent marketing regarding the **"Promise of Genetically Engineered (GE) Foods"** is quite reminiscent of similar praises of DDT and other farming chemicals at the beginning of the Green Revolution. We now know that such toxic compounds ultimately became an absolute disaster to humans and many other species. GE crop engineering has its place in the future, but great caution must be followed to avoid deadly errors and corporate malfeasance against our communities.

2. **Monsanto [now Bayer-Monsanto] is the chief propagator of toxic GMO's** in the world today. Like a vacuum cleaner, it seems to be sucking up all the world's seed stocks and converting fields into Roundup-Ready depositories of their tightly controlled GE seeds and pesticide-soaked crops.

3. **Epicyte is a GE DNA coding** designed to sterilize those who eat corn within which this gene has been inserted. The San Diego based company Syngenta, which produced this "demon seed," openly admits that they used proteins from "anti-sperm antibodies" from the blood of women who had developed allergies to sperm, and inserted these antigen proteins into the genetic coding for their patented products. It is possible that corn being consumed today contains this sperm-killing genome, while current laws do NOT require food manufacturers to disclose GMO contents of their products.

4. **Roundup-Ready crops** have usually been doused with levels of the herbicide, which would not only most likely kill the non-genetically engineered crop species, but it is a **"systemic herbicide"** and thus persists in groundwater as well as within vegetables as well as grain-fed meats consumed by the public. Definitive research has now proven that the primary ingredient in Roundup, **glyphosate** is toxic to friendly bacteria that inhabit the human digestive tract. It is now shown to be damaging to the gut microbiome and immune systems of humans and livestock that consume the toxin.

5. **Food loss & food wastage** are also important issues across the planet. Americans waste some 1250 calories per person daily, an amount sufficient to sustain life in some of the most food desperate parts of the earth. Across sub-Saharan Africa, food loss amounts to some 30% of that produced. This is mainly due to factors for which expanding development is making measurable strides: transportation corridor construction, increase in refrigerated trucking, rural electrification schemes with promises of increase in rural production of fragile agricultural products, cold storage in rural areas, and decreased time in transporting crops to consuming destinations. According to my estimates, reducing the impact of food loss across sub-Saharan Africa by 50% would generate an increased $50 billion in annual income.

6. Increasing reliance upon **Western-style food consumption patterns** across Africa is now reflected in a **rapid rise in rates of chronic diseases** associated with wealthy-nation nutritional consumption. In particular, African diets, like those of their Asian counterparts, now include more meat, dairy, highly processed foods, sugar, salt, fat, and chemical inputs than any previous generation outside of the

wealthy elite that came to dominate the continent during the colonialism phase. Now we see rapid introduction into the metropolitan areas of fast-food restaurants, many of which are franchised as part of powerful multinational corporations. Like these franchises in the host countries, their patrons are increasingly gorging on chemical-laden food, meats with industrial pharmaceuticals, GMO-laden feed, antibiotics, steroids, Prozac-like drugs, and worse. The presence of genetically-engineered crops in this food chain adds a whole other level of paranoia to our cautious perspective. Rates of obesity, cardiovascular disease, diabetes, cancer, and mental illnesses are rising at alarming rates across a spectrum of African metropolises. Cheap and convenient access to fast foods and highly processed foods is something we would be best to interrupt before African hospitals are further overwhelmed by non-communicable diseases (NCD's), just as is the U.S. healthcare system.

7. **Land lease deals, as well as outright land grabs** across Africa are another great source of concern. One such agreement in Madagascar came under intense scrutiny when the South Korean company Daewoo arranged to lease 1.3 million acres of prime agricultural land for a 99-year lease at the shockingly low rate of only 12 cents per acre per year. It was eventually canceled in 2009, and the government which had okayed the deal was put out of office. Despite the cancellation of that contract, the company has managed to maintain a presence in the island nation to further plans to export its crops back to Korea to feed its population.

8. **U.S. and Diaspora-based agricultural experts and producers** have a vital role to play in maintaining the integrity of this anticipated tripling of African agriculture that is being

forecast for the coming decade and more. Key factors toward this growth include:

a. Tapping African nations' rapidly expanding **middle-class consumers** for our products;

b. **Providing export for modern farm equipment**, harvesters, and irrigation systems;

c. **Training U.S. farm professionals** as well as supplying training to African partners;

d. Moving our **agricultural technology professionals** to the continent in large numbers;

e. Providing **safe seed stocks, organic farming supplies,** and expertise to Africa.

f. **Supplying technology for storing, transporting, and producing** finished food products to be manufactured close to areas of rural farm production.

Appendix 2 – Paradigm Shift

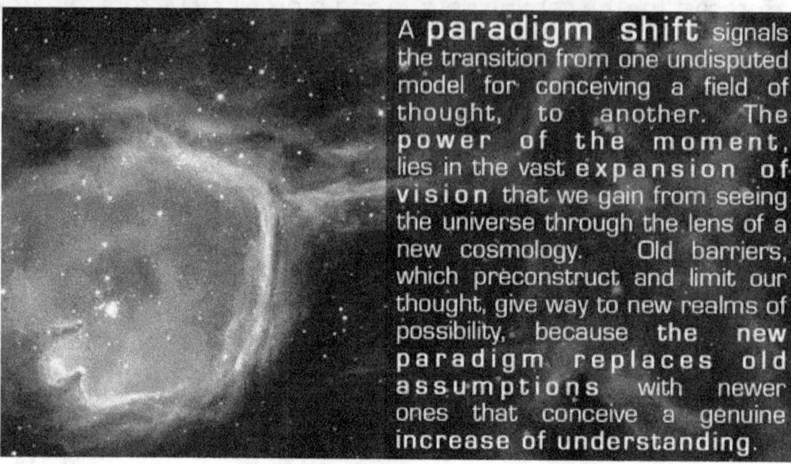

1. Definition- Paradigm: a theory or a group of ideas about how something should be done, made, or thought about

Paradigm Shift — is a dramatic change in the paradigm of a scientific community or a significant change in the fundamental standards of any discipline or group

2. Malcolm X said: "Of all of our studies, history is most qualified to reward our efforts." One hundred years ago and more, the value of Black Labor built the wealthiest agricultural economy that modern history has recorded throughout North and South America and the Caribbean.

3. Our agricultural genius brought rice farming to the U.S., who used our expertise to become a leading rice exporter. Additionally, the imagination of just one black inventor George Washington Carver saved failing southern agriculture when he taught crop rotation, America's first approach to sustainable ecology.

4. A hundred years ago, Blacks controlled nearly six times the amount of farmland than they do today. Historically, African agricultural mastery served as the actual basis of the rise of

human civilization. It was the value of black agricultural and industrial labor that allowed the U.S. to rise to become the wealthiest nation on Earth.

5. After World War One, Blacks fled from terrorism which plagued us in the nation's agricultural south, leaving for industrial centers such as New York, Philadelphia, Washington, Detroit, Chicago, Kansas City, and others, During WWII, it was the value of black labor which allowed this nation to become the economic superpower that rose to dominate the world.

6. Beginning in the '80s, there was a paradigm shift in American capitalism and the pursuit of profits, and corporations betrayed the urban industrial workforce. They shifted manufacturing to areas of the world with low-cost, high-value labor, as well as imported cheap labor into the country primarily to displace the black laborer who was now a more expensive labor reserve.

7. For large numbers of black workers left behind as industry deserted the cities, a new illicit economy rose to displace the sustenance of the previous businesses that had served us for generations. Accompanying the cash flow from drug-fueled escapism came ultra-violence, superstition and fantasy, and the valuation of style over substance; we started faking the funk.

8. Many young people have little understanding of the macroeconomics that drive whole societies. Black youth are being called "redundant labor" and "useless eaters" within the highest levels of power. We cannot risk another generation falling from its former place as the most valuable labor resource in America. We now have the insights, resources, skills, and the opportunity to reverse this degenerating course and recover our power.

9. 17 of the 35 fastest growing economies in the world today are African nations. In just the agricultural sector, it is expected that

it will triple in yearly production to provide $660 billion new dollars for the global economy. In other areas, similar growth is being forecast. How much of those trillions of new global dollars do you plan to deposit into your accounts?

10. Now we see the reason to pool our money, invest in rural properties, build facilities on our land with our trained workforce, create industries from farming to high tech sectors. That is when we will be the primary directors of our economic fate, and then this nation will once again recognize the awesome power of black labor and black wealth.

Appendix 3 – Future Education for African Youth

The future belongs to those who have best prepared to create that future today.

The pace of change in the world today is profoundly affected by several significant trends. These include *megatrends* such as individual empowerment, the diffusion of power, demographic patterns, sustenance, and climate change. As well there are numerous *game-changers* in effect, including a crisis-prone global economy, a spreading "governance gap," war and peace, regional collaboration, and the impact of new technologies.

We must concentrate our efforts to educate both youth and older generations on how to manage anticipated *tectonic shifts* that are upsetting the entire global order and threatening to reverse more than 500 years of global dominance by European powers.

Thus we have researched a broad spectrum of these trends and concluded that the theme of *Africa Rising* would be the most potent and beneficial influence on global development for this and future centuries. Toward participating in and realizing that aim, we must emphasize the following careers for our youth to be raised as the absolute leadership for the future that we wish to create.

15 Critical Careers of the Future

Here is a valuable list of fifteen essential careers of the future for which we should be training our youth to excel:

1. Space-based systems

2. Wildlife management / Nature tourism

3. Child birthing, prenatal care and post-birth support for child and mother

4. Research and development for science, industry, and systems management

5. Biological sciences, neuroscience, and molecular biology

6. Robotics and human-machine interfaces

7. Macro development policy experts

8. Ocean resources development and management

9. Renewable energy specialists and systems engineers

10. Infrastructure development engineers and construction management

11. ICT (Information and Communications Technology) including cybersecurity

12. Agribusiness – from farm to processing and markets

13. Cloud-based banking development and management

14. Mass media, entertainment, and communications production

15. Development investment management

Further Resources

- THE ROAD TO POWER: Seven Steps to an African Global Order – Keidi Awadu, 1999
- THE BLACKEST SOIL: Africa Can Feed the World (A Scientific Roadmap to Agricultural Preeminence for the 21st Century – Keidi Awadu, 2020
- THE REPAIRING: A Practical Plan for Self-Determined Reparations – Keidi Awadu, 2019
- FUTURENOMIC$: Preparing Your Enterprise to Win in the New Global Economy – Keidi Awadu, 2018
- INDUSTRIAL HEMP: Uses and Opportunities – Keidi Awadu, 2017
- THE SUN RISES IN THE EAST: African Growth and Development for the 21st Century – Keidi Awadu, 2014
- KUJICHAGULIA VILLAGES: A Practical Plan for Self-Determination – Keidi Awadu, 2013
- Africa Destiny, Pan African Development – www.AfricaDestiny.com
- Living Superfood (nutrition information) – www.LivingSuperFood.com
- The Conscious Rasta Report – www.Keidi.biz/CRP2012
- Africa for the Africans Tour and Investment Travels – www.AfricaForTheAfricans.org
- The Pan African Agricultural Development Institute – www.PanAfriDev.org
- The Pan African Future Investment Group – www.TheAfricanFuture.com
- Access our daily webcast radio and TV system at www.LIBTV.com

Make sure you check out the latest Conscious Rasta Reports at www.Keidi.biz/CRP2012:

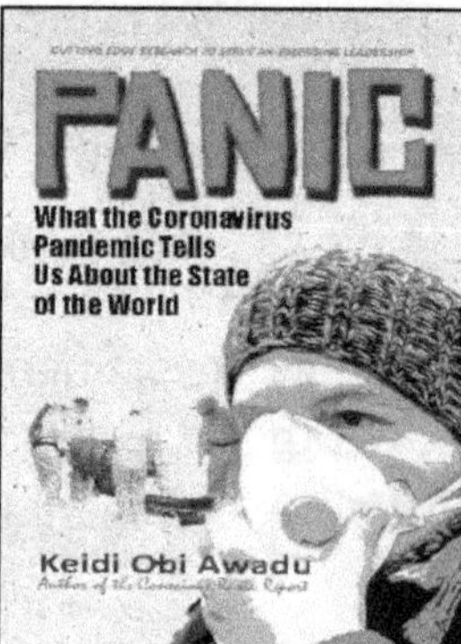

Check out Keidi Awadu daily on LIBRadio.com and LivingInBlack.com
More of these Pan African futurist studies are at AfricaDestiny.com